Queens and Queenship

PAST IMPERFECT

See further
www.arc-humanities.org/our-series/pi

Queens and Queenship

Elena Woodacre

ARC HUMANITIES PRESS

Introduction

Studying queens in the twenty-first century might seem to be flying in the face of modern societal and academic trends. Images of queens consort "standing by their man" or in the shadow of their husband could be seen as nearly an affront to feminist ideology. Studying "women worthies" or famous figures from the past could also be understood as running counter to modern historical approaches which have sought to break down "great man" studies and instead focus on the lives of everyday men and women rather than well-known elite figures. Monarchy itself is seen by many as an outdated institution, a relic of the past even, and therefore somehow backward looking to focus on. Given these prevailing sentiments, what then is the point of studying queens in this day and age?

A deeper understanding of queenship studies and indeed of queens themselves, allays these potential concerns. In many ways, nothing could be more appropriate in our modern era, influenced by feminism and ideals of gender equality, than studying women who were politically active and incredibly influential in their own time and beyond. Indeed, many queens—whether ruling in their own right, on behalf of children and spouses or co-ruling with them—were important political leaders who often challenged the patriarchal frameworks of power and demonstrated that women could be effective rulers, leading the way for today's modern female politicians. Queenship studies challenges androcentric narratives and debunks notions of "great man" political history which tends to focus on particular kings and their reigns by emphasizing the historical practice of co-rulership and corporate monarchy, where rule was enacted collectively with both men and women involved, even if only one man often bore the title and crown. Indeed, studies of regnant queenship have shown that female rule was more common than often assumed, as succession practices and situational factors opened up opportunities for ruling queens not only in Europe but in Africa, India, China, and even on the Arabian Peninsula. Monarchy itself has continued to exist and evolve in line with the changes in society itself over millennia. While many of today's monarchs may not have the absolute power of their predecessors, many of them are female, including the long-reigning Elizabeth II of the United Kingdom. Royal succession laws have also been evolving in step with modern ideas of gender equality to allow equal primogeniture, ensuring that the rights of female royal children are protected and that reigning queens are not just a result of the absence of a direct male heir.

Finally, queenship studies offers not just a greater understanding of obvious or elite figures—looking at queens opens up a wider network of men and women from the relationship of queens with subjects and tenants who sought her assistance and influence, to the men and women of their household from stable boys and household clerks to seamstresses and damsels of the chamber, her officials and stewards who could be spread across the realm as well as artists, artisans, architects, and more who owed their livelihood to the queen's commissions. This wide web of relationships is central to the practice of queenship and opens up a myriad of potential protagonists to examine, from the very highest to the very lowest of social status—it is not just about the woman at the centre.

Thus, queenship is a complex and exciting area of study which is firmly in step with modern interests in gender and a challenge to, not a product of, traditional historiography. This book's purpose is to give the reader a thorough grounding in queenship studies, from its earliest beginnings to current themes and theories and directions for future research as well as examining key aspects of the queen's office and the role she played in the function of monarchy and the wider history of her realm and period. Due to the slim nature of this volume, the intention here is to give an intensive overview rather than create a comprehensive textbook. While not every possible situation or scenario can be brought to the fore, the ideas will be illustrated by relevant examples from the premodern period with not only more familiar European figures but those from various geographical and cultural settings. In addition, restrictions of space mean that the full context of every queen's life or the history of particular dynasties used as examples cannot be given here, yet it is hoped that these tantalizing glimpses will encourage readers to learn more about figures and cultures less familiar to them. Taking a *longue durée* and global approach to queenship is vital in order to gain an understanding of the variability and constants of the queen's role over time and place, as well as the impact of different cultures and religions. Each of the main chapters of this book will focus on one of three core aspects of queenship: Family, Rule, and Image. The first chapter will examine the importance of family, both a queen's natal dynasty and the family she marries into as well as the family she creates through maternity. The second chapter looks at aspects of rulership, including co-rule with husbands and children as queens consort and regent as well as female succession and the particular situation of regnant queens. The final chapter will focus on a range of activities which were central to not only the practice of queenship including image creation, ceremonial, and patronage. For queens, the personal and the political were always deeply entwined, as each of these chapters will demonstrate.

Studying Queens

Before these core aspects are addressed however, it is important to begin with a quick overview of the field of queenship itself in order to understand the particular perspective that scholars in the field bring to the study of queens and royal women. Key debates and ideas will be foregrounded here which will inform the discussion in the following chapters as well.

The lives of queens have been studied and written about, both individually and collectively, for centuries. Collective biographies in particular played an important role in keeping the interest in and memory of premodern queens in the public eye, from Boccaccio's *Famous Women* up to the Strickland sisters' popular *Lives of the Queens of England*.[1] Queenship studies as an academic discipline emerged out of the wider movements of women's and gender history, even though it draws on scholarship and specialists from a number of different areas such as literature, art history, archaeology, cultural studies, and political history. One of the earliest key works in the field of queenship studies, which was also important for beginning to define the idea of queenship itself, was Marion Facinger's 1968 piece "A Study of Medieval Queenship."[2] Facinger argued that the power and influence of Capetian queens steadily declined over this period, reducing the queen's role to being that of a dynastic broodmare and largely ceremonial. While Facinger's argument that the queen's official role had been diminished by the reorganization of royal households and the development of administrational apparatus has been subsequently challenged, her examination of the practice of queenship itself and the notion of the queen's office was important for the field. These two elements have become central to the development of queenship studies—that the early interest in biographical studies of

---

1 On the role of collective biography on the development of queenship studies see Elena Woodacre, "Well represented or missing in action? Queens, Queenship and Mary Hays," in *The Invention of Female Biography*, ed. Gina Luria Walker (London: Routledge, 2017), 21–36.

2 Marion Facinger, "A Study of Medieval Queenship: Capetian France, 987–1237," *Studies in Medieval and Renaissance History* 5 (1968): 3–48.

particular women has become fused with a wider examination of the theory and practice of queenship and a desire to understand the mechanisms of the queen's office.

Facinger was not the only scholar to suggest the notion of diminishing power for royal and elite women in Europe during the high and later Middle Ages. Moving forwards into the 1970s, 80s, and 90s where there was increasing research into women's studies generally as well as queenship specifically, influential work by McNamara and Wemple as well as the French historian Georges Duby reinforced Facinger's hypothesis of a law of diminishing returns for royal women's authority.[3] They argued that the apogee of female power occurred around the first millennium and declined over the eleventh and twelfth centuries, leaving late medieval women in a significantly reduced position compared to their foremothers. However, later generations of feminist historians and queenship scholars have questioned this paradigm and the notion that female power was wielded rarely and only by "exceptional" women, resulting in a series of roundtables, conferences, and publications which have worked to demonstrate the constant presence and trajectory of female authority throughout the Middle Ages and beyond.[4] Indeed, queenship

3 Jo Ann McNamara and Suzanne Wemple, "The Power of Women through the Family," *Feminist Studies* 1 (1973): 126–42; Jo Ann McNamara, "Women and Power through the Family Revisited," in *Gendering the Master Narrative: Women and Power in the Middle Ages*, ed. Mary Erler and Maryanne Kowalski (Ithaca: Cornell University Press, 2003), 17–30; Georges Duby, "Women and Power" in *Cultures of Power: Lordship, Status and Process in Twelfth-Century Europe*, ed. Thomas N. Bisson (Philadelphia: University of Pennsylvania Press, 1995), 69–88.

4 See the output of two roundtables which debated the notion of declining power at the medieval congresses at Kalamazoo and Leeds in a special issue of *Medieval Feminist Forum* 51, no. 2 (2016) and the output of the 2015 "Beyond Exceptionalism" conference, *Medieval Elite Women and the Exercise of Power, 1100–1400: Moving beyond the Exceptionalist Debate*, ed. Heather Tanner (New York: Palgrave Macmillan, 2019).

scholars are still exploring the nature of power and debating over the use and understanding of the terminology that we use to describe it—unpicking the use of "power," "agency," "influence," and "authority." While all of these terms are important and useful to describe the activities of queens, Theresa Earenfight has noted that we tend to use the term "power" more often with kings and "agency" with women, thus possibly diluting or tacitly underplaying their role.[5]

Terminology has been a challenge even with regard to the terms "queen" and "queenship" itself. As I have discussed elsewhere, these terms have significantly different meanings in different languages which can reflect different understandings of the role of royal women in dynastic government.[6] For example, the English word "queen" etymologically stems from a term which specifically refers to the wife of a king, whereas Romance languages use terms which derive from the Latin *regina* which is the female form of *rex* or ruler, rather than denoting a consort's role. Taking a global perspective makes terminology even more complicated as there is no clear or simple equivalent of "queen" in languages such as Arabic for example. Different monarchical structures also make it challenging to simply equate the European model of "queen" to the position that other royal women held in other geographical and cultural contexts. In some polygynous models there may be no one clearly identified as a "queen" or even a chief or principal wife like the ancient Macedonian court. Confusion can be caused when titles which equate to queen are used for multiple women in the royal family as seen in high medieval Portugal or the use of *basilissa* by Ptolemaic daughters as well as wives. In spite of these issues,

---

5 Theresa Earenfight, "A Lifetime of Power: Beyond Binaries of Gender," in *Medieval Elite Women*, ed. Tanner, 271–94.

6 Elena Woodacre, "Introduction: Placing Queenship into a Global Context," in *A Companion to Global Queenship*, ed. Elena Woodacre (Bradford: Arc Humanities, 2018), 1–12. See also Stefan Amirell, "Female Rule in the Indian Ocean World (1300–1900)," *Journal of World History* 26, no. 3 (2015), 443–89 at 446–49.

given the lack of a universal equivalent, or until one is developed, we can still use the terms "queen" and "queenship" to discuss and explore the role of royal women across time and place, as long as it is used with these caveats in mind and not as an attempt to generalize the experience of all women or to brand all cultures inaccurately or insensitively with a European framework.

With all these challenges in terms of how we conceptualize and describe the queen's role, how do we approach the study of queenship? Sources can pose a difficulty as the role of royal women has often been minimized, obscured or even omitted in administrative or official documents, annals and histories and even material culture, whether deliberately or subconsciously.[7] A further hurdle can be the survival of sources—while this is always a challenge for premodernists in particular, it can be exacerbated by archival practices, where the sources relating to kings and male members of the dynasty can be prioritized for retention over that of royal women who are seen as less central to the function of government. Indeed, in rare cases even material culture relating to particular queens can be destroyed in an attempt to erase their memory, for example Henry VIII's work to remove traces of Anne Boleyn's brief tenure as queen of England in the decoration of Hampton Court and other royal residences after her execution in 1536. Queenship scholars, like all scholars of women's and gender history, have sought to read between the lines of existing sources and gain clearer perspectives by collecting and comparing all existing sources in order to counter the androcentric master narrative and reinsert these women into political and monarchical history.

Part of this effort has been raising awareness of the practice of corporate monarchy—while there has been an excessive focus on the individual who wore the crown, in reality a "reign" is the product of a group of people who rule with, or

---

7 Theresa Earenfight, "Highly Visible, Often Obscured: The Difficulty of Seeing Queens and Noble Women," *Medieval Feminist Forum* 44, no. 1 (2008): 86–90.

even in place of, the royal figurehead. This concept of monarchy as a "flexible sack" which can accommodate a varied number of individuals including rulers, consorts, favourites, lovers, advisors, and dynastic members of both sexes is vital to understanding queenship.[8] As we will discuss in chapter two, queens were co-rulers, sharing power in formal roles as consorts and regents and less formally as members of the dynasty—as mothers, sisters, daughters, aunts, and cousins. Regnant queens too were co-rulers, as all monarchs are, sharing power with their consorts, lovers, and relatives in the same way as their male counterparts. Even unmarried regnant queens, like the well-known "Virgin Queen" Elizabeth I of England, ruled with favourites, including William and Robert Cecil, Francis Walsingham, and Robert Dudley. The balance of power might be shared out relatively equally or be heavily weighted in favour of one individual, be it ruler or any member of the ruling coterie. This group can be a simple partnership of two individuals—a royal couple, ruler and favourite, mother and child—or it can be as large a group as the ruler desires, or needs require. Yet, the role of women as a part of this ruling group or partnership has often been overlooked, in part due to the understated way in which queens often engaged in co-rule. Their influence on their partners was often exercised in private, through their relationship with the ruler, be it their spouse, child, or sibling and thus was rarely documented and can be hard to identify or quantify. While some women did publicly and explicitly demonstrate their authority, others were equally powerful but far more discreet as a "power behind the throne" or behind the screens which often separated Muslim and Asian royal women from the public.

---

8 For this "flexible sack" theory, see Theresa Earenfight, "Without the Persona of the Prince: Kings, Queens and the Idea of Monarchy in Late Medieval Europe," *Gender and History* 19, no. 1 (2007): 1–21.

Expectations of Queens and Ideals of Queenship

A queen was clearly a crucial part of the mechanism of monarchy, not only as a co-ruler, a representative of her natal family and a dynastic progenitor as we will discuss in chapter one. She was also the premier woman of the realm and as such had a great responsibility to project and conform to ideals of queenly and female behaviour as an example to all others. In Korea, the queen was the "state mother" and as the official exemplar to all the women of the kingdom, her behaviour was considered to be vitally important—indeed King Seongjong in his *Annals* claimed "The rise or fall of a state is linked to the demeanor of the queen."[9] Her conduct was thus closely scrutinized and any deviation from expectations could evoke not just criticism but could lead to her downfall. Seongjong defended his divorce and deposal of his wife Yun for her "transgressions" and "lack of virtue" from her plotting to eliminate rivals in the royal harem, arguing she had to go as "She is incapable of being a model for the royal ancestors above or for the people below." A queen's perceived failure to conform to queenly ideals could also have a catastrophic impact on her husband, as the case of Marie Antoinette aptly demonstrates. While the French Revolution was caused by many factors, the queen's failure to craft and project an image that resonated positively with her subjects and satisfied their expectations of queenly behaviour contributed to the downfall of the monarchy. In the final chapter, we will explore the vital importance of image creation in order to demonstrate a queen's adherence to societal ideals of queenly behaviour and queenship itself.

These societal ideals and expectations can be gleaned from a variety of sources. In the same way as the literary genre of "Mirrors for Princes" which advised heirs to the

---

9 *The Annals of Seongjong* in Shin Myung-ho, *Joseon Royal Court Culture: Ceremonial and Daily Life*, trans. Timothy V. Atkinson (Seoul: Dolbegae, 2004), 125.

throne and current rulers of how to rule effectively and behave in an appropriately kingly manner, there were also "Mirrors for Princesses" such as the *Speculum dominarum* written by Durand de Champagne for his patron, Juana I of Navarre, at the turn of the fourteenth century. "Mirrors" for both kings and queens exhorted them to exhibit an extensive list of qualities that were often impossible for a mere mortal to possess in order to exercise the queen's office well and be an effective model to all other women of the realm. These advisory guides could also be less formal in nature—just as Emperor Charles V wrote an advisory tract for his son Philip II of Spain on how to be king, Charles's sister Catalina of Austria, Queen of Portugal, wrote a similar piece for her daughter, Maria Manuela, when she married Philip II in 1543. This advisory piece instructed Maria on how to navigate the Castilian court and how to be a queen, advising her to emulate the late Empress, Isabel of Portugal, who was revered as a model of Iberian queenship. Nor were "Mirrors for Princes" or princesses a purely European phenomenon—advisory guides for royal men and women can be found in Islamic and Asian culture as well, including the fifteenth-century Empress Xu who wrote her "Instructions for the Inner Quarters (or *Neixun*)" as a set of moral teachings and guide for the Imperial wives and concubines.

Conduct literature, aimed at women generally to communicate gender ideals and desired behaviour could be scaled up to court and royal women. Indeed, many of these books which advised women on appropriate behaviour were written by court "insiders" such as Ban Zhao's *Lessons for Women* or Christine de Pizan's *Treasure of the City of Ladies: Or the Book of the Three Virtues*. While some conduct books explicitly counselled royal women on their behaviour, such as Pizan's frequent admonitions to the "good princess" others did so more subtly. Even tracts ostensibly aimed at a wider female audience still demonstrated what was expected of queens and royal women—as the premier woman of the land, a queen was expected to be a paragon of virtue and therefore the perfect woman. As William Caxton noted his description of the ideal queen in the late fifteenth-century *Game and Playe of the Chesse* "she is above all others in estate and reverence so she should be an example to all others."[10]

Yet another way in which ideals of queenship can be gleaned is through histories and literary sources, particularly collective biographies. The examples given by the lives of queens and royal women of the past were used to demonstrate how one should, or should not, behave—creating "worthies" or historical examples that later women were encouraged to pattern themselves on or "anti-worthies" who served as salient examples for the repercussions of poor womanly or queenly conduct. These "anti-worthies" or negative examples of the past, powerful women who were demonized like Cleopatra, Wu Zetian, the Merovingian queen Fredegund, or Catherine de Medici were often used by detractors of female rule to demonstrate the destructive impact of bad queenly behaviour—resulting in the downfall of rulers, dynasties, and the destruction of the realm. These historical, or even legendary, examples of great queens of the past gave royal women patterns to copy, or models to avoid which could endure for centuries or even millennia in the case of Liu Xiang's *Biographies of Women* which was written in the first century BCE but "remained influential into modern times."[11] Indeed the preface to the section of this work which features biographies of the "Worthy and Enlightened" specifically addresses queens, noting that "Consorts and empresses who attend to these phrases/Will bring to their names lauds and praises."[12]

---

10 William Caxton, *The Game and Playe of the Chesse*, ed. Jenny Adams (Kalamazoo: Medieval Institute Publications, 2009), 27 (modernized English above by me).

11 Robert Joe Cutter and William Gordon Crowell, "Women in Early Imperial History and Thought," in *Empresses and Consorts: Selections from Chen Shou's Records of the Three States with Pei Songzhi's Commentary* (Honolulu: University of Hawaii Press, 1999), 44.

12 Anne Behnke Kinney, trans. and ed., *Exemplary Women of Early China: The Lienü Zhuan of Liu Xiang* (New York: Columbia University Press, 2014), 25.

The Empress Xu in her "Instructions for the Inner Quarters" also urges her readers, the Imperial wives and concubines, to pay heed to these biographical "worthies" by "taking the ancients as models and trying to emulate them."[13]

While gender roles and expectations of womanly behaviour are subject to variation over time and in different cultural settings, there are some ideals of queenship which are nearly universal in a historical context. For the purpose of condensing these down into a memorable and concise framework, these can be summarized or categorized into the following "four goods" and "three Ps." As well as being the ultimate "good woman" and a model of virtuous behaviour as discussed previously, queens were also expected to be good wives, good mothers, and good rulers. In addition, they were expected to be pious, peacemakers, and pretty. This may be a brief and seemingly trite summary, but the following discussion aims to flesh out these overriding principles of queenly behaviour.

Queens were expected to be a model of virtue to their household, court, and subjects. This notion of virtue encompassed all of the positive traits and behaviours that contemporary women were expected or encouraged to possess. In her *Enseignements* Anne of France (or de Beaujeu), daughter of Louis XI and virtual queen as regent for her brother Charles VIII in the late fifteenth century, advised her daughter Suzanne to "devote yourself completely to acquiring virtue [...] whatever you do, above all, be truly honest, humble, courteous and loyal."[14] These same traits were expected of queens, including—surprisingly perhaps—humility. Christine de Pizan in her chapter "How the good princess will wish to cultivate all virtues" begins by advising this princess to particularly "cultivate earthly humility." Pizan urges the princess

---

13 Empress Xu, "Instructions for the Inner Quarters (*Neixun*)," in *Sources of East Asian Tradition*, vol. 1, *Premodern Asia*, ed. William Theodore de Bary (New York: Columbia University Press, 2008), 427.

14 Anne of France, *Lessons for my Daughter*, ed. and trans. Sharon L. Jansen (Cambridge: Brewer, 2004), 31.

to remember that God reigns supreme and that "she is a poor mortal creature, frail and sinful and that the rank that she receives is only an office for which she will soon have to account to God."[15] Part of this humility is the princess's modest behaviour: Pizan notes that the good princess "will behave respectfully and speak softly [...] greeting everyone with lowered eyes." The courtier Ban Zhao's *Lessons for Women* also equates humility and modesty with ideal behaviour. She urges her reader to "control circumspectly her behavior; in every motion to exhibit modesty [...] to speak at appropriate times; and not to weary others (with much conversation)."[16] Durand de Champagne in his advisory "Mirror" also emphasized the need for queenly humility, advising her to listen and learn meekly and quietly, avoiding frivolous conversation.[17]

The next chapter "Family" will engage with the ideal that queens must be good wives and mothers. Given the centrality of marriage and maternity to queenship, many texts advised royal women on this aspect of their lives. Queens, like all women, were expected to be good wives—the aforementioned quality of humility was part of this role. The seventeenth-century Japanese writer Kaibara Ekiken advised women of the ruling samurai class that "In her dealings with her husband, both the expression of her countenance and style of her address should be courteous, humble and conciliatory."[18] Pizan also advised the princess to be humble

---

15 Christine de Pizan, *The Treasure of the City of Ladies or the Book of the Three Virtues*, trans. Sarah Lawson (London: Penguin, 2003), 19. Subsequent quotations are from this translation.

16 Ban Zhao, "Lessons for Women," in *Images of Women in Chinese Thought and Culture: Writings from the Pre-Qin Period through the Song Dynasty*, ed. Robin R. Wang (Indianapolis: Hackett, 2003), 184–85.

17 Rina Lahav, "A Mirror of Queenship: The *Speculum dominarum* and the Demands of Justice," in *Virtue Ethics for Women 1250-1500*, ed. Karen Green and Constant J. Mews (New York: Springer, 2011), 37.

18 Kenneth G. Henshall, *Dimensions of Japanese Society: Gender, Margins and Mainstream* (New York: Palgrave Macmillan, 1999), 14.

towards her husband as her lord and to "love her husband and live in peace with him, or otherwise she will have already discovered the torments of Hell" (24–25). Ban Zhao warned against excessive love between man and wife, arguing that excessive time in one another's company will lead to lust and licentiousness. This may have been a coded reference to the emperor's relationship with his wives and concubines, as Chinese annalists often equated the excessive interest of emperors in their imperial harems with poor government and the destruction of reigns.

Yet even more important than restraining male lust was the necessity for the queen to remain chaste. Chastity was held up as a key ideal of womanhood by many societies. The Romans emphasized three key qualities for women: *constantia*, *fides*, and *pudicitia* (steadfastness, loyalty, and chastity or sexual virtue). The latter was particularly prized, indeed while chastity could not make a Roman woman a queen, it could bring her a crown—a *corona pudicitiae* which was awarded to those women who remained chaste and loyal to only one husband over the course of their life. Female chastity was equally prized by the Chinese, as this short segment of the influential *Classic for Girls* (or *Nüerjing*) illustrates:

> First of all a woman's virtues
> Is a chaste and honest heart,
> Of which modesty and goodness and decorum
> form a part.[19]

While chastity was a prized quality for women generally for queens it was absolutely essential. As dynastic progenitors, the queen's chastity was paramount to ensure the purity of the royal line, particularly in monarchical systems based on hereditary succession. William Caxton's description of the ideal queen in *The Game and Playe of the Chesse* appears to

---

19 Anon., "Classic for Girls (Nüerjing)," in *Images of Women in Chinese Thought and Culture: Writings from the Pre-Qin Period through the Song Dynasty*, ed. Robin R. Wang (Indianapolis: Hackett: 2003), 442.

be nearly obsessed with the concept of chastity—it is mentioned no less than five times in his short overview of the "forme and maners of the quene" (26–31). It is the first quality mentioned in his list of qualities that a queen must possess, it is then repeated again with two anecdotes which underline the importance of queenly chastity, next he returns to it with his description of her manners and comportment, noting that it is impossible for a queen to be appropriately "shamefast" or modest without also being chaste. This connection may well reflect the fact that the root word of the aforementioned Latin term *pudicitia* for chastity is *pudor* which equates to "a sense of modesty." The final two mentions are with regard to the queen's children, noting that she must encourage her sons and daughters to "kepe chastité entirely." Caxton argues that chastity is also vital to becoming a queen, "for we rede of many maydens that for their virgynyté have ben maad quenes," citing the case of two princesses who used rotting chicken flesh to prevent being raped by invaders and were later rewarded by becoming queens of France and Germany. Just as Caxton instructed queens to keep their children chaste, Chinese empresses were responsible not only for their own chastity but was charged with finding chaste women for the Imperial harem, to ensure that the emperor had a plethora of virtuous women to choose from to ensure the continuation of the royal line.

The link between chastity and royal succession can also be seen in what could be called the "fear of Guinevere." This legendary queen was a staple of medieval romances, as the Arthurian tales had considerable reach and longevity across Western Europe and beyond. Guinevere could be seen as an "anti-worthy" or cautionary tale for other queens or princesses preparing for queenly life who might be reading the saga of how not to behave. Even if Guinevere's behaviour was not explicitly criticized in many versions of the Arthurian tales, she illustrates two of the greatest concerns about a queen— that she might be barren and unchaste. Indeed, Guinevere's failure to bear an heir for King Arthur and her affair with his greatest knight, Sir Lancelot, are arguably at the heart of the fall of Camelot. Other cautionary tales of legendary queens whose lack of chastity brought down rulers and realms can be seen in the tale of the Songstress Queen of King Dao of Zhao in the *Biographies of Women* or in the life of the infamous Roman empress Messalina who flagrantly engaged in illicit affairs and was killed for reportedly plotting to overthrow her husband and make her lover the new emperor.

The importance of motherhood, for queens and indeed women generally, can also be seen in religious texts and traditional proverbs. These foundational elements of society and culture are also another way through which ideals of queenship can be communicated. The high value placed on motherhood and resulting respect and reverence for mothers can reinforce queenly authority, particularly as queen mothers and regents. This can be seen in Islam for example, where the often-quoted story from the Hadith of the Prophet Mohammed's thrice repeated insistence that one should serve and be dutiful to one's mother—before he answered that one should also serve one's father. African societies also deeply value the role of mothers—the Yoruba proverb that "Mother is Gold," sums this idea up succinctly. In chapter three, we will discuss how Islamic and African monarchies accorded powerful positions, indeed arguably the most powerful position for royal women, not to consorts but to queen mothers—reflecting how these societal values can be translated into monarchical practices.

Ideals of queenly motherhood can also be communicated through religion in more direct ways. For example, in the sixteenth century John Calvin wrote a commentary on the Book of Isaiah in the Old Testament of the Bible which he addressed to the ruling queen Elizabeth I of England. In his commentary, he stressed a particular passage from Isaiah (49:23) "And kings shall be thy nursing fathers and their queens thy nursing mothers." While this passage does clearly reinforce the idea of queenly motherhood, Elizabeth was unmarried and thus had no children of her own. Calvin used this passage instead to reinforce the idea of sovereign duty, that a queen could be a mother to her people in a larger sense, rather than just a dynastic progenitor. The accession of another regnant English queen Anne Stuart in 1702 also drew heavily on this verse from Isaiah and reinforced the idea of queenly "nursing mothers," both in the sermon given by John Sharp, the Archbishop of York, and in Jeremiah Clarke's coronation anthem which deliberately emphasized the word "queen" in his musical setting for this biblical verse.[20] While Anne too was a mother in the metaphorical rather than biological sense as her seventeen pregnancies had failed to produce a surviving heir to the throne, she could also leverage this biblical verse to reinforce her position as a queenly mother to the nation. Biblical verses and figures, such as Deborah, the Judge of the Israelites, were used to express queenly ideals and reinforce female authority but conversely were also used by detractors of gynecocracy, such as John Knox, in an attempt to undermine a queen's position. For every Deborah and Esther who were used to demonstrate ideals of queenship, "anti-worthies" like Jezebel, queen consort of Ahab who was demonized for her extravagance and worship of false prophets, could be held up as warnings of the negative repercussions of queens who failed to conform to the high expectations of queenly conduct.

In addition to being good wives and good mothers, queens were also expected to be good rulers. As discussed above, the duty of a queen to look after her people as well as her own children was highlighted. A key element in this was wisdom, which can be seen as a central focus in the aforementioned "Mirror for Queens," the *Speculum dominarum*. Durand de Champagne's work was based, like Calvin's commentary for Elizabeth I, on biblical verse—in this case on Proverbs 14:1, "The wise woman builds her house." Here the queen is the wise woman and her house is the kingdom; wisdom gives her good judgement and virtue enables her to be an effective co-ruler with her husband. The Chinese *Nü Sishu* also empha-

---

20 Matthias Range, *Music and Ceremonial at British Coronations: From James I to Elizabeth II* (Cambridge: Cambridge University Press, 2012), 112–13.

sizes the importance of queenly wisdom in creating a success-ful ruling pair by listing examples of the sage judgments and actions of early empresses before concluding, "Therefore, is it not simply true that since the ancient times all accomplished great emperors must have had wise empresses?" (Wang Xiang, 225). In addition to these textual works, another way to demonstrate ideals of queenship and queenly behaviour is through visual images. Several examples of late medieval illustrated manuscripts from the French court, including the *Jeu des echecs moralisés*, the *Livre du gouvernement des roys et des princes*, and the *Grandes Chroniques de France* use visual depictions of the queen and royal couple to reinforce the ideal of queenly wisdom, stressing her role as wise counsellor to her husband and able educator of her royal children.[21] Indeed many queens were very well educated themselves, including Elizabeth I who was a renowned linguist, as well as many other contemporary royal women both in Europe and in Safavid Iran.

Having discussed the expectations that queens should be good women, wives, mothers, and rulers, we turn now to three further qualities that royal women were expected to possess: being pious, peacemakers, and pretty. The first quality of piety is central to queenship in multiple cultures. In one Islamic "Mirror for Princes," the *Kutadgu Bilig* advised rulers to "choose a wife for her piety," urging them to "find a good and God-fearing woman."[22] In Christian Europe, queens modelled themselves in terms of their projected image and religious activities, subconsciously or overtly, on the Virgin Mary, or Queen of Heaven. The lives of saints, some of whom like St. Margaret of Scotland were queens themselves, could also provide models for pious queens to emulate, in the same way as biographies of other women "worthies." This can also be seen in tales of the lives of Islamic sufi saints or mystics

---

21 See Cécile Quentel-Touche, "Charles V's Visual Definition of the Queen's Virtues," in *Virtue Ethics*, ed. Green and Mews, 53–80.

22 See Marina Tolmacheva, "Female Piety and Patronage in the Medieval Hajj," in *Women in the Medieval Islamic World*, ed. Gavin R. G. Hambly (New York: Palgrave Macmillan, 199), 173.

as "hagiographies relay messages about the proper or per-haps ideal behavior of women," emphasizing devotion to God, prayer, poverty, and charity.[23]

The latter activity, charity, became a key way for queens to demonstrate piety—perhaps one which they, as women with considerable means at their disposal, were particularly suited to. Christine de Pizan discusses charity and piety extensively in the *Treasure of the City of Ladies* and devotes an entire chapter to "the habits of pious charity that the good princess will cultivate." Pizan argues that a queen must engage in charity as a means of wealth redistribution as "you have received more plentifully than many others" and notes that the good princess must be "ever mindful of this principle so that she may accomplish works of mercy, although she may be well established in her grandeur, preserves the virtue of her station" (24–25). Pizan advises the princess that she should work with her almoners to give money to the poor and go out to visit hospitals and those in need herself, setting "a good example to those who see her perform such work and with such humility, for nothing influences the common people so much as what they see their lords and ladies do." This idea of the public performance of piety was a vital part of the exercise of queenship in Christian Europe, from regularly attending services at court and in towns and cities as well as engaging in religious festivals and rituals, such as washing the feet of poor women during the Royal Maundy in England. While their Islamic counterparts may not have been able to publicly perform piety in the same manner due to the seclu-sion of royal women in the harem or zenana, they were able to engage in acts of patronage which carried strong mes-sages about royal women's piety and charity out across the realm. Examples of the demonstration of piety and charity by queens will be discussed further in chapter three.

In addition to counselling the good princess to be pious and charitable, Christine de Pizan also highlights another of

---

23 Ruth Roded, *Women in Islamic Biographical Collections* (Boulder: Rienner, 1994), 94.

the ideal qualities of a queen—to be a peacemaker. She links a queen's peacemaking abilities to her "pure, mild and holy charity" which makes her the ideal mediator and argues that "This work is the proper duty of the wise queen and princess: to be the means of peace and concord, to work for the avoidance of war because of the trouble that can come of it" (21–23). Pizan not only considered the queen's peacemaking qualities theoretically, she wrote two letters directly to her patron, Isabeau of Bavaria, Queen of France, urging her to use these qualities to broker a peace between the rival factions in the royal family which were threatening the stability of the realm.[24] The senior women of the Mughal dynasty were also expected to broker peaceful resolutions to dynastic disputes, while younger women could be offered in marriage as a means of seeking peace with neighbors and erstwhile rivals. These peacemaking activities: intercession, brokering peace treaties and queens' roles as players and pawns in matrimonial diplomacy, will be revisited in the following two chapters. A further type of peacemaking which was seen as vital for queens in polygamous monarchical structures, was keeping peace within the harem. One of the reflections on "queenly virtue" in the *Mao Commentary* was that a good empress was able to create peace in the palace through ensuring harmony among the wives and concubines.[25] Peace and order at the heart of the dynasty and court were absolutely crucial to the stability of the realm; thus the efforts of queens and empresses to keep peace between members of the royal family, the women of the court and harem and rival factions, would have a wide-ranging impact.

Finally, queens were expected to represent contemporary ideals of beauty and were often portrayed or described in idealistic manner, even if their actual appearance was not

---

24 See Tracy Adams, "Recovering Queen Isabeau of France (c.1370–1435): A Re-Reading of Christine de Pizan's Letters to the Queen," in *Fifteenth-Century Studies, 33*, ed. Edelgard E. DuBruck and Barbara I. Guisick (Rochester: Camden House, 2008), 35–54.

25 McMahon, *Women Shall Not Rule*, 30–33.

necessarily as attractive. Contemporary ideals of beauty vary greatly over time, place, and culture, yet just as a queen was meant to be the ultimate woman in demonstrating all the expectations of female behaviour, she was also meant to reflect ideals of beauty in her appearance and dress. Indeed, Caxton begins his description of the ideal queen by claiming "She ought to be a fayr lady sittyng in a chayer and crowned with a corone on her heed"—the very first quality he attributes to her is being fair or beautiful (26). Ideals of queenly beauty can also be seen in the descriptions of queens in the medieval Welsh Triads—some of these literary works describe queens as "the most beautiful women ever seen."[26] Indeed, it has even been argued that "Beauty [...] was a cultural requirement for a queen," using the example of Elizabeth I who "had to nurture and sustain the legend of her beauty" as a means of ensuring the continuing loyalty of her courtiers and subjects, and as a vital element of the myth of Gloriana.[27] If beauty was a means of security for a regnant queen like Elizabeth, it was equally important for consort queens. Alfonso X of Castile in his *Siete Partidas* argued that beauty was a key element in selecting a royal bride as "The more beautiful she is, the more he will love her, and the children which he has by her will be more handsome and more graceful; which is very fitting for the children of kings, in order that they may make a good appearance among other persons."[28] In this way, many of the elements discussed above as the ideals of queenship are tied together as Alfonso argues

26 Danna R. Messer, "The Uxorial Lifecycle and Female Agency in Wales in the Twelfth and Thirteenth Centuries" (PhD diss., Bangor University, 2014), 132.

27 Anna Riehl, *The Face of Queenship: Early Modern Representations of Elizabeth I* (New York: Palgrave Macmillan, 2010), 45–46.

28 *Las Siete Partidas*, ed. Samuel Parsons Scott and Robert I. Burns. 5 vols., vol. 2 *Medieval Government: The World of Kings and Warriors (Partida II)*, ed. Scott and Burns (Philadelphia: University of Pennsylvania Press, 2012), 298 (Title 6), available online at muse. jhu.edu/book/21372.

that being beautiful will make a queen a good wife, a good mother, and the ideal woman, and a positive example as the foremost female in the realm.

Taken together, these ideals of queenship form a useful foundation for a wider consideration of queens. In the following chapters, we will test these ideals and expectations against examples of the practice of queenship by women from various kingdoms and cultures across time and place. Understanding what was expected of royal women gives us a framework for exploring the queen's office which will be fleshed out by the realities of individual women's experience of queenship in the chapters that follow.

Chapter 1

Family

Family and matrimony arguably defined the role of a queen in multiple ways. A woman was initially defined by her origin or membership of a particular family or royal dynasty. For consort queens, her position itself was created through marriage—as noted previously, the etymology of the word "queen" itself indicates being the ruler's wife. For all queens, consort or regnant, there was considerable expectation that she would produce an heir to continue the family's hold on the throne, or possibly adopt or select an heir if she could not produce one biologically. Fundamentally, queens operated within the milieu of the family, sitting at the nexus of her natal family, her marital family, and the "nuclear" one she created with her husband.

This chapter focuses on the centrality of family to both the lives of individual queens and the practice of queenship itself. It traces the lifecycle of queens, noting how their engagement with the family changed over their lives. We will begin with a queen's natal family, examining the education of royal women and preparation for queenship as well as the selection of a spouse who could bring a potential advantage to her own dynasty. Then we will focus on the crucial transition that consort queens make between their natal and marital families, looking at how they adjust to a new environment and build a personal and political partnership with their new husband. The next stage, creating a family, highlights the vital role that maternity played in the practice of queenship, ideally fulfilling the role of dynastic progenitor which made royal women the pivotal link between one reign and the next. Finally, the chapter contemplates the role of the matriarch or female head of the family—arguing that this period of the lifecycle can potentially be the peak of a queen's power.

One of the major issues that this chapter addresses is the key differential in royal matrimonial structures which have a major impact on this element of queenship—monogamous vs polygamous systems. We explore the impact of these two systems with regards to each of these stages in a queen's lifecycle and to the effect that monogamy and polygamy (or more specifically polygyny) had in terms of the role of women vis à vis both the ruler and the royal family. The consequent effect on the maternal aspect of the queen's role is addressed, highlighting the way in which having multiple sexual partners for a male ruler created a potential plethora of heirs and also removed the focus on the queen as the sole vehicle for ensuring heirs for the dynasty.

The Formation of a Queen

A queen's early years are often the least documented of her life as royal woman. Indeed, most junior royals, apart from the heir apparent, are often given little attention by national and dynastic histories and chronicles, apart from mentions of their birth. More information on the childhood experience of princesses comes from financial records, where expenses for ceremonial to celebrate their birth, payments for household members and servants, and records of gifts can often be found which can enable us to begin to construct some understanding of these foundational years. We can also begin to understand the preparation involved for their queenly role from records associated with the payment of tutors which illuminate the formal element of a queen's education to some extent. However, it is important to understand that royal women were prepared for queenship in several ways—in addition to formal education and training in various skills such as musicianship and dancing, they were also prepared more informally through interaction with the women of the royal household and other family members. It is also important to remember that training for women who were entering a polygamous system was somewhat different to that of European women being prepared for the queen's role. For example, a young female *jariye* (slave) in the Ottoman *Enderûn* (or Inner Service or Court) had to work her way up through all of the various stages of training, learning to read, given religious instruction, was taught musical skills, to sew, and grounded in all court ceremonial and protocol. While this education was not entirely dissimilar to princesses preparing to be queens in Europe and would have been similarly desirable skills for members of harems and inner palaces in India or Asia, a *jariye* was not being individually educated or groomed for a particular role, just given a foundation which could lead her in multiple trajectories within the *Enderûn*.[1] Ultimately however, the focus was the same for all royal or palace women—it was vital that they picked up the required skill set, learning, and understanding for both the role which they would ultimately occupy and the courtly milieu they would be living in whether it was as "the" queen or one of many royal wives or concubines.

"On-the-job" training was another way of preparing a princess to become a queen. In terms of an heiress, having the opportunity to share rule with her predecessor, often a father, was a golden opportunity to prepare for regnant queenship. Indeed, it was common for both male and female heirs to learn rulership by co-ruling with their predecessor, administering a particular area of territory on their own or even the realm itself in the temporary absence of the ruler. Blanca I of Navarre is an excellent example from the fifteenth century—her elder sister Juana briefly served as regent during the absence of their father Carlos III while she was heir to help her prepare to rule full time. Later Blanca worked closely with her father when she became heiress after her sister's untimely death—the

---

1 Lesley Peirce, *The Imperial Harem: Women and Sovereignty in the Ottoman Empire* (Oxford: Oxford University Press, 1993), 139–42.

king specifically noted some decisions had been made due to her counsel. As queen, Blanca entrusted her own heir, the Príncipe de Viana, to rule in her absence, for example when she went to Castile for the wedding of her daughter to the kingdom's heir or when Blanca was on pilgrimage. Isabel of Portugal is another example of learning the queen's role, this time that of a consort, by doing it. After her mother Philippa of Lancaster died in 1415, Isabel stepped into her mother's shoes, becoming the first lady of the realm and fulfilling nearly all of her mother's functions.[2] This enabled her to step smoothly and successfully into her marital role as Duchess of Burgundy and run the elegant Burgundian court with aplomb. Learning via "osmosis" by watching their mothers, stepmothers, aunts, and mothers-in-law, was another key mode of preparation which, while difficult to quantify, should not be underestimated. Certainly, Isabel of Portugal's close observation of her mother's effective queenship enabled her to take her mother's place and later run her own court and household.

Even "surrogate" mothers can be powerful role models who could play a crucial role in a queen's formative years. Take, for example, the interesting linkages at the French court in the early Renaissance. Anne de Beaujeu, the daughter of Louis XI and sister-regent for Charles VIII, not only wrote the aforementioned *Enseignements* for her own daughter Suzanne, she played a key role in the development of her brother's fiancée Margaret of Austria, who lived at the French court as a young bride-to-be. Later when that marriage was broken off, she helped the young queen Anne de Bretagne adjust to life at court and learn her new queenly role. Anne's household in turn became famous as a sort of finishing school for royal and elite women, not only preparing them for lives as queens and noblewomen in terms of formal education,

---

2 See Manuela Santos Silva, "Princess Isabel of Portugal: First Lady in a Kingdom without a Queen (1415–1428)" in *Queenship in the Mediterranean: Negotiating the Role of the Queen in the Medieval and Early Modern Eras*, ed. Elena Woodacre (New York: Palgrave Macmillan, 2013), 191–205.

learning court etiquette and the accoutrements expected of them but making the matches which secured their place in society. Anne's own daughters Claude (Queen of France) and Renée (Duchess of Ferrara) benefited from this super-lative educational environment as well as Carlotta, Princess of Naples, and Anne's Foix cousins Anne (Queen of Hungary and Bohemia), Germana (Queen of Aragon), and Françoise (later mistress of Francis I of France). Margaret of Austria took the training she received at the French court from Anne de Beaujeu and insights that she gained from her mother-in-law, Isabel I of Castile, to create a glittering court of her own as regent in the Low Countries. Here she played a key role in the formation of several queens, including raising her nieces Eleanor (Queen of Portugal and France), Mary (Queen of Hun-gary and later Margaret's successor as regent), and Isabella (Queen of Denmark) as well as other women who received a polish from being in her cosmopolitan household like Anne Boleyn, later Queen of England.

As well as learning from observation and informal training from mothers or maternal stand-ins, we can also see queens taking an active hand in their daughters' formal education. In this same period, we can see Isabel of Castile taking a strong role in the education of her daughters as well as her son and heir, Juan. Isabel employed Italian humanists Antonio and Alessandro Geraldino as well as a female Latinist, Beatriz Gallindo, for her children. Not only was Isabel keen for her daughters to learn Latin, a skill she herself felt the lack of in the early years of her reign, but they learnt multiple lan-guages to prepare them not only for the countries that they might come to reign in but to be conversant with ambassa-dors and foreign visitors. Indeed, the impressive education that her daughters received clearly prepared them well both for the practice of queenship and to living up to the high ide-als expected of them as queens:

> Our age has seen the four daughters of Isabel, whom I mentioned a little earlier, each of them well accomplished. People in various parts of the country tell me in words of praise and admiration, that Queen Juana, wife of Philip and

mother of our Emperor Charles, answered in Latin to the Latin ex tempore speeches that are customarily delivered in in every town in the presence of new princes. The English say the same of their queen Catherine, sister of Juana. All say the same of the other two sisters, who met their death in Portugal. There were no women in human memory more chaste than these sisters, none with a more unblemished name, and there have been no queens who were so loved and admired by their subjects [...] none fulfilled to such perfection the ideals expected of the virtuous woman.[3]

The writer of this passage was Juan Luis Vives, who was brought to England by Catherine of Aragon to tutor her own daughter, Mary I. Mary's excellent education became not only a good foundation for her eventual rule but a basis for her deep friendship with her stepmother Katherine Parr, Henry VIII's last wife. Mary and Katherine shared a mutual interest in the work of Erasmus and Mary's own knowledge of Latin and rhetoric was enhanced by their mutual study of Erasmus's translation of the New Testament and other contemporary works. Katherine Parr in turn played an important role in the formal education of Mary's half-siblings, Edward VI and Elizabeth I, as well as Lady Jane Grey, who briefly became queen in 1553. Both Catherine of Aragon and Katherine Parr arguably served as important models of female rule in their successful regencies during Henry VIII's campaigns in 1513 and 1544; Parr's regency was one which both Mary and Elizabeth would have been able to observe at close hand which may have helped them both prepare for their own tenures as regnant queens.[4]

---

3 Juan Luis Vives, *De institutione feminae christianae*, ed. C. Fantazzi and C. Matheeussen (Leiden: Brill, 1996), 36–39.

4 Elena Woodacre, "Between Regencies and Lieutenancies: Catherine of Aragon (1513) and Kateryn Parr (1544)," in *Les alters ego des souverains. Vice-rois et lieutenants généraux en Europe et dans les Amériques (XVe-XVIIe siècles)*, ed. Philippe Chareyre, Álvaro Adot, and Dénes Harai (Presses de l'Université de Pau et des Pays de l'Adour, 2021), 185–206.

Marriage and Matrimonial Strategies

Ultimately, the investment in the education and preparation of daughters was important to the family in terms of either preparing the next ruler if she was an heiress or producing an eminently marriageable potential consort queen. Royal women were incredibly important as a means of crafting alliances between families which could bolster or improve the dynasty's position. The Hapsburg family of Austria demonstrates how a savvy matrimonial strategy can have a huge impact on the upward trajectory of the dynasty, as reflected in the oft-quoted motto *"Bella gerant alii, tu felix Austria nube* (Let others fight, you, Austria, marry)!" However, it is also important to note that the marriages of royal women were not only politically significant, they were also a vital means of cultural exchange, which will be explored in chapter three. While the matrimonial value of princesses as potential brides can be seen across all periods and cultures, the strategies of individual families varied significantly and often shifted over time or in response to changes in the often turbulent political landscape.

When considering the options of families for marrying their daughters, there were a series of choices to consider, each of which has particular potential consequences or opportunities for the family. The most basic and fundamental of these options could be summarized in a very simple way as in/out or up/down. In or out, or endogamy versus exogamy, could be considered in multiple ways. Endogamy, or marrying within the group could be seen at various levels. In its most limited sense, this means marrying within the royal family itself, even within the normally accepted boundaries of close kin, such as brother–sister marriages which were common in dynasties across the world from Hawaii, ancient Egypt, the Inca, some kingdoms in Southeast Asia, and several African royal families. Endogamy has some dynastic advantages in terms of ensuring the purity of the royal bloodline and keeping resources in the family. In terms of a princess, it allows her to practise isogamy as well, that is a marriage of equals— if she is marrying within the realm, no one else could be of the same rank unless they are a member of her own family.

There are disadvantages as well—clearly marrying within the family would seem to preclude the possibility of contracting external alliances through marriage which could be politically beneficial. However, polygynous societies, where royal incest is more prevalent, can get around this by making a sister the principal wife and queen while still allowing the king to contract more marriages and thus alliances. The other obvious disadvantage of marrying within the family is the potential impact on the health of the offspring through interbreeding. Many of the societies which practise brother-sister marriages, such as the Ankole, Buganda, Bunyoro, Zande, and Shilluk dynasties of Africa, stipulate that these marriages remain sterile or are unconsummated. Again, as they are polygynous societies, there is no pressure on the queen herself to act as the sole dynastic progenitor as the king has multiple wives who can produce royal offspring. However, the consequences of extensive endogamous marriages can be seen in the powerful Hapsburg dynasty in Europe. This royal family used marriages between close kin to keep territory and political power within the dynasty—this strategy became even more important in the late sixteenth and seventeenth century to keep the family politically united when the Spanish and Austrian Hapsburg dominions were separated after the abdication of Emperor Charles V in 1556. The lineage of Ana of Austria, Queen of Spain, is an excellent example of how this strategy operated. Her maternal great-grandmothers, Juana of Castile and Catalina, Queen of Portugal, were sisters and her maternal grandparents, Emperor Charles V and Isabel of Portugal, were thus first cousins. Her mother, Maria of Spain, married her first cousin, Emperor Maximilan II, and Ana herself went on to marry her uncle, Philip II of Spain, in 1570. By the end of the seventeenth century, the Spanish Hapsburg line failed when the extremely sickly Charles II, the result of generations of Habsburg endogamy, was unable to produce any issue with either of his two wives.

In the wider sense, a princess could marry outside the royal family but within the realm, empire, or sphere of influence of her family. This did mean that she would be "marrying down" or practising hypogamy. Within the realm, this could mean marrying into the nobility which could benefit the royal family's hold on power by solidifying their alliances with other key families within the realm. The potential disadvantage is that these noble families could become in turn competitors for the throne by using the royal blood acquired through these matches to press a matrilineal claim to the crown. The English "Wars of the Roses" is an example when various strands of the extended Plantagenet royal family, like the Mortimers which had received several infusions of female royal blood, had rival claims to the throne. However, the Aztecs are an example of how "interdynastic hypogamy" could be a very effective political strategy, by marrying their daughters to subordinate rulers so that their daughters became principal wives or queens of the subordinate king and her son, the heir to that throne.[5] This had the impact of strengthening the alliance and reaffirming the loyalty of subordinate rulers to their overlord through ties of marriage and blood.

However, many families sought to "marry up" or practise hypergamy by contracting matrimonial alliances with their daughters which elevated or raised the status of their family by connecting it with a stronger or more powerful dynasty. There was huge potential for the noble or elite family of a royal bride to acquire political influence and power through her exalted rank, even more so if her child became the next ruler. The examples of the Boleyns and Seymours, who both had queens emerge from their ranks in the mid-sixteenth century are useful examples of the rise and fall of queenly families. The Boleyns experienced a huge surge of influence at court and the acquisition of new titles and positions for family members when Anne Boleyn became Henry VIII's obsession and then his bride in 1533. However, they also experienced a familial catastrophe when Anne and her brother George were both executed in 1536, leaving their stock at court severely

---

5 See Lori Boornazian Diel, "Till death do us part: Unconventional Marriages as Aztec Political Strategy," *Ancient Mesoamerica* 18, no. 2 (2007): 259–72.

depressed until Anne's daughter Elizabeth ascended the throne in 1558. When Jane Seymour replaced Anne in 1536 and bore the long awaited male heir the following year, her family gained a long term advantage—although Jane died in the aftermath of childbirth, they had considerable goodwill at court as the family of the heir apparent. Later, Jane's brother Edward was able to parlay his familial relationship as Edward VI's uncle into becoming the Lord Protector in the early years of Edward's reign before he fell from power in a coup d'état and was executed in 1552. The Chinese were very aware of the potential for excessive interference from the families of an empress and tried various strategies to attempt to control their influence. The Wei, who took power in the third century CE, noted the chaos in the later Han dynasty, when a series of families of empresses had caused political mayhem at court. To combat this, an edict was issued in 222 CE which forbade any family members of an empress consort or dowager from playing any role in the government and stipulated that they would no longer be awarded a noble rank—seriously restricting the potential advantages that her family might gain from hypergamy.[6] In Japan, the Shogun chose a queen consort or *midai* from the nobility—while their marriage formed an important political bond with her family, the fact that concubines, rather than the *midai* normally bore the Shogun's children may reflect a deliberate strategy to avoid increasing the power of the *midai*'s family by making them relations of the heir, potentially giving them influence over the next Shogun.[7]

Marriages between royal families were a vital way of building and maintaining alliances, and they have been intensely studied in terms of premodern Europe for their impact on politics as well as cultural exchange. Often these marriages, while outside the realm, were with other nations which had a common religion, culture, or ethnicity, such as the mar-

---

6 McMahon, *Women Shall Not Rule*, 110.

7 Tracy Adams and Ian Fookes, "Queens and Courtesans in Japan and Early Modern France," in *A Companion to Global Queenship*, ed. Woodacre, 285–98 at 287.

riages between the Manchus and Mongols in the seventeenth century to reaffirm both their alliance and shared cultural heritage. However, in the same century, the example of the brides of the Stuart dynasty demonstrate the difficulties of marrying outside their religious group. The Catholic queens Henrietta Maria, Catherine of Braganza, and Mary of Modena all suffered considerable criticism due to their religion which put them at odds with their largely Protestant subjects in a period when confessional differences were a source of great tension and conflict in Europe.

However, some dynasties chose not to marry their daughters at all and kept them instead either within the family or commit them to a religious life. In early medieval Europe there were several families who used this strategy including the Ottonian dynasty in the Holy Roman Empire and that of Anglo-Saxon Wessex. In both areas, princesses frequently entered into nunneries like Wherwell, Romsey, Gandersheim, and Quedlinburg where they often became powerful abbesses, wielding considerable influence on behalf of their families in both secular and ecclesiastical politics. A similar but slightly different strategy was used during the same period in the Iberian kingdom of León. However, the Leonese princesses became consecrated virgins, rather than nuns or abbesses, and became *domina* of a large collection of religious and secular properties and lands which became known as the *Infantazgo*. Lucy Pick has argued that the decision not to marry these royal daughters was strategically valuable as it ensured that the princesses were solely focused on supporting and promoting the fortunes of their natal family, instead of transitioning to her husband's or producing children who might challenge her brothers or nephews for the Leonese throne.[8] Moreover the princesses' control of the *Infantazgo* increased the reach of the royal family, improving their connection with and control of the realm through their

---

8 See Lucy Pick, *Her Father's Daughter: Gender, Power and Religion in the Early Spanish Kingdoms* (Ithaca: Cornell University Press, 2017).

administration of the territory and the networks they built with tenants and nobles who served as officials on their lands.

One of the most famous unmarried queens is Elizabeth I of England, who resisted intensive pressure from her council to contract a matrimonial alliance and used the possibility that she may or may not marry as a means of balancing European politics during her reign. However, while this strategy proved successful for her, the majority of regnant and consort queens were married at least once. This brings us to the matrimonial situation for regnant queens—in what ways was it similar or different to the experience of princesses or women destined to be a consort? As a brief summary of what I have discussed at length elsewhere, the choices are exactly the same in terms of marrying in or out (endo/exogamy) or up or down (hyper/hypogamy) but the ramifications are somewhat different.[9] Marrying within the kin group, in terms of a cousin, could be an effective strategy for a female heiress as it could potentially stem the challenge of a male rival. This worked well for Mary II and her husband and cousin William of Orange—their combined claim to the English throne gave them the wherewithal to supplant her father James II in the "Glorious Revolution" of 1688. However, Giovanna I of Naples had rather disastrous results with the majority of her four marriages, particularly those to her cousins Andrew of Hungary and Louis of Taranto who both sought to wield power and push her aside. Indeed, as will be discussed further in the following chapter, this was the constant danger for many regnant queens—that their husbands would rely on patriarchal frameworks of power and authority to insist that their conjugal supremacy should translate into ruling in place of, rather than beside, their wives. While marrying within the kin group would give a queen a relatively equal marriage to a man of suitably royal blood, marrying within the realm itself would

---

9 See Elena Woodacre, "The Queen's Marriage: Matrimonial Politics in Pre-Modern Europe," in *Marriage in Pre-Modern Europe: Italy and Beyond*, ed. Jacqueline Murray (Toronto: Centre for Reformation and Renaissance Studies, 2012), 29–46.

entail hypogamy, forcing her to look downwards for a noble husband who might engender jealousy at court by raising him above his station to become her king consort.

Marrying outside the kin group or realm had its own set of opportunities and dangers. For true isogamy, or a marriage of equals, a regnant queen could marry another male monarch. This could be an excellent strategy to potentially unify two realms under a personal union or long-lasting merger such as in the case of the *Reyes Católicos*, Isabel I of Castile and Ferdinand II of Aragon, whose marriage in 1469 started a golden age in Spain or the marriage of Jadwiga of Poland and Jagiello of Lithuania, whose union in 1386 created the largest realm in medieval Europe. However, the marriage of Juana I of Navarre and Philip IV of France in 1284 shows a different side to this scenario—in their case Juana remained with her husband in Paris and her kingdom was ruled in absentia and in line with the interests of France with little sympathy for the needs and traditions of the queen's Iberian subjects. Marriage to a foreign prince or noble could again be troublesome if her husband was more interested in the needs of his own lands than her realm, unless he was forced to sign away his rights to his own patrimony like Fulk of Anjou, king consort of Jerusalem, or Francis of Lorraine, husband of Maria Theresa of Austria. A landless prince or younger son could be a better option—at least this worked successfully for Queen Anne and her husband George of Denmark, who was content to be his wife's subject and was not distracted by territory or claims of his own.

While a regnant queen had the luxury of remaining in her own familial home, consort queens generally had to make a transition from her natal family to her marital one, unless she was one of the Egyptian, Hawaiian, or African queen-sisters that were discussed previously. This transition could be a challenging one—if she was marrying down for example, she might struggle to adjust to the change in rank. The Aisin Gioro of China combatted this potential issue by co-opting their daughters' husbands into the Imperial dynasty, literally and figuratively, making them part of their family rather than the princesses joining that of their husbands.[10] Even if a queen was marrying "up" or across to another royal family, there was still a process of transition to be negotiated, in terms of adjusting to a new position and an unfamiliar court which often entailed learning new customs and a different language. While this process could entail a physical change, such as adjusting her hairstyle or fashion to fit in with a new court, some women deliberately chose to import styles of dress from their homelands as a way of signalling their allegiance to their natal families, as will be discussed later. A more radical way to attempt to sever the connection between a queen's previous existence and family was to change her name. The women who became wives of the Oba, or ruler, of Benin were given a new name by her husband and it was forbidden to refer to her by her old name once she entered his harem.[11] Queens who changed religions as well as families, may be required to change their name when they were accepted into a new faith, such as Catherine II of Russia who was born Sophie Friederike Auguste von Anhalt-Zerbst-Dornburg but became Catherine or Ekaterina Alekseyevna on her baptism into the Orthodox church in 1744.

However, this connection with a queen's natal family could be both an advantage and disadvantage to her in her husband's court. On the positive side, she was the physical representation of the political bond between the two realms or families, which could be to her benefit—at least when the relationship with the two was stable or the alliance was considered beneficial to both parties. If her position and standing was strong in her marital court, she could work to promote not only good relations between the two families but could

10 Shuo Wang, "Qing Imperial Women: Empresses, Concubines and Aisin Gioro daughters," in *Servants of the Dynasty: Palace Women in World History*, ed. Anne Walthall (Berkeley: University of California Press, 2008), 137–58 at 152.

11 Flora Edouwaye S. Kaplan, "Politics in an African Royal Harem: Women and Seclusion at the Royal Court of Benin, Nigeria," in *Servants of the Dynasty*, ed. Walthall, 115–36 at 125.

potentially advance the fortunes of her natal dynasty and those from her native land. Maintaining a connection with her natal family could give her support in her new homeland when things became difficult; for example, Catherine of Aragon's powerful nephew Emperor Charles V was a formidable ally to her cause when Henry VIII sought to end their marriage. However, queens were often suspected of placing her natal family's needs in front her new marital home. This suspicion could be well founded as demonstrated in the Aztec *Anales de Cuauhtitlan* which features two tales of royal women acting as spies for their natal family's benefit—the princess Chalchiuhnenetzin who informed her brother of her husband's planned rebellion and the daughter of Tecocoatzin who not only informed her father of her spouse's military movements against him, she even set fire to the temple in her husband's capital city as the battle between the two began (Boornazian Diel, 269). Yet maintaining a connection to her natal family could also be a very positive aspect politically—for example, the queen mother or *namasole* of Buganda (in present day Uganda) played a vital role in cementing the link between the king and her clan, ensuring both the promotion of her own family and their support for the king, their kinsman.

Some queens struggled to make this transition from her natal to her marital family, particularly if she came from a foreign land. Apart from the natural homesickness she might experience, a queen might find it difficult to learn a new language and integrate with the members of her new court and household. The retention of household members from her native land could ease this transition in some ways by providing plenty of familiar faces who spoke the same language and understood her cultural heritage and background. However, it could also slow down a queen's integration into her new marital court and family, becoming a source of tension at court as her attendants could be seen as a barrier to accessing the queen who were monopolizing the lucrative and prestigious positions in her household. A queen's foreign attendants could also be seen as potential spies or foreign political agents and an unnecessary drain on the crown's expenses, which could lead to the expulsion of household members. This situation can be seen in England in repeated calls for purges of foreigners in Joan of Navarre's household in 1404, 1406, 1416, and 1426 as well as the dismissal of most of Henrietta Maria's French attendants in 1626. This could be a distressing situation for a queen—having already experienced the loss of her natal family when she left home, sending home the members of the virtual family of her household could make her homesickness and isolation in her marital court even more acute.

One way to ease the shift from natal to marital family was effective education and preparation—as noted previously this was designed to train a princess for the life she would lead as queen and if it was specifically targeted with her new destination in mind, for example by teaching her the language of her marital court, this could make the transition easier. Personnel from the court that a princess was set to marry into could also help—Margaret of Austria sent one of her ladies and some fashion advice from the Burgundian court to help Henry VIII's sister Mary prepare for her planned move to the Low Countries to marry Margaret's nephew Charles (later Emperor Charles V). Margaret of Austria is also an example of another strategy for easing the transition between natal and marital courts as she was dispatched to the French court of her betrothed Charles VIII as a child as noted previously, where she was known as "*la petite reine* (or little queen)," ostensibly ready after years of living in her marital home to take on the queen's mantle when she came of age. Yet Margaret and Mary are also examples of the potential pitfalls of these preparation strategies—both of their betrothals fell apart and they were ultimately redeployed to different marital destinations which made their preparation for these particular marriages and court settings redundant.

Preparation for life in a new royal court could be even more challenging without the process of betrothals which often entailed a considerable period before marriage in which a bride might be able to prepare for her new life ahead, assuming the match came to fruition. It could also be very challenging, for example in the case of the Joseon queens of Korea who were selected through a lengthy and intensive screening process which whittled down an initial pool of all eligible girls of the same age across the realm through a series of rounds to find the chosen bride. The selection process for some royal brides was seemingly or even deliberately random, such as the bride shows used in Russia in the sixteenth and seventeenth centuries and the Northern Wei dynasty of China who used metal divination to select the next empress. Both of these selection methods were contrived to eliminate any notion of favouritism of a particular elite family or jockeying at court to try to make a daughter the next empress by the seemingly random choice of who might take the fancy of the tsar or the mystical input of a diviner. Another way to avoid any dissension between the elites of the realm over a choice of a royal bride was to put the selection process in their hands. In Africa, the Lotuho, Lulubo, and Loyoka kings (Sudan and South Sudan) had their wives chosen by the *monyomiji* or the elders/elites of the kingdom—they would bring her to the king to see if he would accept her and if he did, then the traditional bridewealth would be paid.[12]

The Particularities of Polygamous Courts

In terms of polygamous monarchies, a woman might be recruited into the harem or inner palace by several different means, most of which offered little chance for the woman to prepare for this transition into the royal court. Women could arrive in the harem through a number of routes: as a slave who was purchased or war booty, through a drafting mechanism such as the tri-annual system used by the Qing dynasty in China or by being gifted to the ruler by one's own family. The latter was perhaps one of the most common routes of entry, particularly for wives rather than concubines,

---

12 Simon Simonse, *Kings of Disaster: Dualism, Centralism and the Scapegoat King in Southeastern Sudan* (East Lansing: Michigan State University Press, 2017), 225.

and was used in the same way as matrimonial alliances—to strengthen the bond between a ruler and the various families within the realm and/or subsidiary rulers. This could be a voluntary gift or a requirement; for example, in Thailand the families of provincial administrators had to send a female relative into the royal harem as a pledge of their loyalty to the crown. In Buganda, the strongest clans were obliged to send wives for the king and the king had the right to demand wives from the chiefs at any time.

It is important to reflect further on the practices of royal monogamy and polygamy and the impact that this had on the queen's wifely role and on queenship itself in these different systems. We often conceptualize queenship within the framework of monogamy, in a Christian, European sense. Monogamy defined the queen's role as "the" king's wife, his female counterpart and "other half." With only one wife, the queen is not only the king's ruling and personal partner but the mother of the next ruler whose maternal role will ensure the continuation of the dynasty, blending the bloodlines of her natal and marital families. Monogamy was encouraged by the Christian church in the early and high Middle Ages in Europe, this emphasis and the concurrent development towards systems of royal succession which increasingly favoured male primogeniture put more focus and weight on the queen as the potential mother of sons to ensure a pure and unbroken line of descent from revered dynastic ancestors such as Charlemagne and St. Louis of France. Yet, prior to this development, there had been a long history of polygyny, concubinage, and multiple forms of marriage in Roman, Welsh, Scandinavian, and Germanic laws. Indeed, long after monogamy had been the accepted norm for European monarchies, many male monarchs continued to have mistresses, some of which were publicly recognized like the official *maîtresse-en-titre* in the French Renaissance court. Indeed, some royal mistresses were able to effectively take the queen's place, either edging her out or dampening the queen's influence as François I's mistress Anne de Pisseleu did to his second wife Eleanor of Austria or as Charles II of England's mistresses did to a lesser extent to Catherine of Braganza. A mistress could even take the position of queen itself as in the case of Anne Boleyn and Catherine I of Russia, wife of Peter the Great.

Just as we can see rivalry between queens and mistresses in the context of monogamous royal systems in Europe, the competition between women was even more intensive in the context of polygynous courts. This competition was centred on power and influence and focused on rising in rank and favour in the harem, zenana, or inner palace by becoming either the queen/empress/principal wife, the ruler's favourite, and/or the mother of the heir—it is vital to note that all three of these prized slots may or may not be held by the same woman. Indeed, the most important and powerful woman in the harem may not hold any of these positions—as we will discuss shortly, it could well be the ruler's mother who held the greatest female position in the realm.

Ranking systems were a key part of polygamous courts— this gave order and structure to the harem or inner palace, which could contain hundreds or even thousands of women. While systems of rank could lead to competition to improve one's position, a lack of rank of position for royal women could arguably make their situation worse, giving them no solid status and making them insecure as they were completely dependent on the whim of the ruler as to whether they or their children were currently in favour to give them any standing at court. Leaving aside the position of the queen mother, which will be discussed shortly, often there was only one woman who held the highest title of queen/empress or principal wife, but the ruler might have many wives, as well as concubines or even servants who were sexually available to the ruler as well. Buganda offers a good example of the strata of royal women—at the top was the queen mother (*namasole*) and the queen sister (*lubaga*). After them, there were three tiers: the titled wives (*abakyala*) which included the chief wife (*kaddulubaale*), the favourite wife (*kabejja*), the *ssaabaddu* who settled internal disputes between the wives and ruler, and the *nassaza* who came from the ruler's paternal grandmother's clan and protected the king's hair and nail cuttings so that they could not be used against him by magical means.[13] After the titled wives came the untitled wives or *abasebeyi* whose sons could still be legitimate royal heirs and the lowest rank was the king's women or *abazaana*.

The Chinese system under the Zhou (ca. eleventh to third centuries BCE) had a fairly similar tripartite system with principal wives, secondary wives, or consorts and concubines. However, this fluctuated under later dynasties; for example, under the Han (third century BCE to third century CE) the number of ranks grew to fourteen before being slashed to three and then expanded again as the number of women in the Inner Palace grew into the thousands. Under the empress dowager and empress there were high-ranking titles like "Beautiful Lady," "Glamorous Beauty," and "Illustrious Visage," right down to the lowest ranking women who had titles such as "Respectful Maid" and "Night Attendant".[14] Ranking was not only important in terms of the pecking order and respect but had a clear financial impact in terms of the woman's financial allowance and resulting privileges, such as better housing. Attracting the attention and favour of the ruler was a key method of improving one's standing and rank in the harem or Inner Palace—in the Ottoman harem the Sultan's favourite was known as the *haseki*. The career of Hürrem Sultan, sometimes known as Roxolana, is a case in point as she was able to rise from being a slave to being the *haseki*, ultimately breaking the trend of unmarried sultans by becoming Suleiman the Magnificent's wife, effectively a queen, and the mother of several of his children.

---

13 Laurence D. Schiller, "The Royal Women of Buganda," *The International Journal of African Historical Studies* 23, no. 3 (1990): 455–73 at 469.

14 McMahon, *Women Shall Not Rule*, 63.

The Importance of Motherhood

After leaving one's natal family and moving to become part of a husband's family and court, the next step was ostensibly to create a "nuclear" family by bearing children. Indeed, the importance of bearing children is something that unites queens and royal women in both monogamous and polygamous court systems. There was considerable pressure on women to produce an heir who would become the next ruler and continue the dynastic line. In monogamous systems, particularly the aforementioned emphasis on hereditary succession and primogeniture in many European monarchies, there was a subsequent focus on a queen as the king's sole wife, to bear an heir to the throne—preferably male. Failure to do so could end the dynasty's rule and lead to a succession crisis or even civil war between potential claimants. A queen's own future was ostensibly under threat if she did not produce an heir as Wladyslaw of Bohemia successfully petitioned to end his marriage to Beatrice d'Aragona in 1500 by accusing her of sterility—she had no children by her first husband, Matthias Corvinus of Hungary either. There was also considerable pressure on Charles II to end his marriage to Catherine of Braganza as his many illegitimate children made it very clear that their own childless union was not due to any reproductive issues on his side. The failure to produce a son was also considered one of the "seven divorceable sins" in Joseon culture as well (Shin, 125).

Yet in polygynous courts, there was less pressure on the queen or empress to produce an heir—in fact, as noted previously, some queens, particularly those married to close relatives like the aforementioned African sister-queens in Ankole, Buganda, Bunyoro, Zande, and Shilluk were not expected to have sexual relations with their brother/spouse and not allowed to produce children. The children of the *coya*, or sister-queen of the Inca emperor, were preferred as heirs, but if she had no children or produced only daughters, then a suitable heir could be selected from any of the sons that the emperor had with his other wives, as long as those wives also had suitably royal lineage (i.e., were sisters, half-siblings, or cousins). In most polygynous systems, heirs could potentially come from any of the ruler's wives or concubines—sometimes these were restricted by rank like the Inca where the royal wives could produce heirs but those of foreign concubines were ineligible or in Buganda, where the children of the lowest ranked women or *abazaana* could not succeed to the throne. This potential plethora of heirs meant that there was far less pressure on queens and empresses in polygynous marriages to bear children; indeed they could adopt the sons of lower-ranking wives and concubines, even after their husband's death, or wider members of the royal, or their own, family. Two examples of dowager queens who made the most of adoption can be found in the queens of Choson (Joseon) Korea who adopted sons to manage the succession and assure their role as queen mother or in the case of multiple widowed queens in Nayaka South India in the seventeenth and eighteenth centuries who used adoption to ensure their continued rule under the guise of regency.[15]

Motherhood was not just important for ensuring the dynasty's future, it ensured a royal woman's future as well. For a queen in a monogamous situation, motherhood gave her security and an added stake in the fate of her marital family. This could directly translate into political power as was the case for Maria Carolina, Queen of Naples, who gained access to the State Council in 1775 when she gave birth to the heir to the throne, as had been stipulated in her matrimonial contract.[16] Being the mother of the heir also ensured that a queen would continue to have an important position at court after the death of her husband—indeed that position could become even greater if she became regent for an underaged

---

15 See Seokyung Han, "Dowager Queens and Royal Succession in Premodern Korea" and Lennart Bes, "The Ambiguities of Female Rule in Nayaka South India Seventeenth to Eighteenth Centuries," in *A Companion to Global Queenship*, ed. Woodacre, 195–208 and 209–32.

16 See Cinzia Recca, "Maria Carolina and Marie Antoinette: Sisters and Queens in the Mirror of Jacobin Public Opinion," *Royal Studies Journal* 1, no. 1 (2014): 17–36 at 21 and 23.

ruler, meaning that a queen could move from being merely consort to being the effective sovereign of the realm, as will be discussed in the following chapter.

The rewards of motherhood could be equally beneficial to women in polygynous courts. For low-ranking women in the Japanese Ooku, bearing the Shogun a child meant an immediate improvement in housing, as they were given their own room—this was the ultimate achievement for a concubine in a contemporary board game called "Success in Serving in the Inner Quarters."[17] For a slave in an Islamic harem, becoming the mother of a ruler's child or an *umm al-walad*, was a route to freedom—her children would not only be free but could become heirs to the throne, enabling her to gain power and standing as the mother of a future sultan or even as his regent, if he was underaged when he came to the throne. For wives and concubines of all ranks, motherhood was an opportunity to either maintain or gain influence and power as the mother of the next ruler. This led to a great deal of competition within the harem or Inner Palace—particularly when succession practices allowed a great deal of flexibility in terms of which of the ruler's offspring could succeed and a plethora of sexual partners meant that the ruler had a large number of potential heirs. One way that the Ottoman court attempted to minimize the competition between potential heirs, and the resulting fratricide which was an unfortunate by product of several sultans' accessions, was to limit each concubine to one son each. This was monitored by the sultan's mother, the *valide* sultan, who was in charge of the harem and had a role in selecting the women sent to her son's bed in order to control royal reproduction. While this meant that each concubine who was lucky enough to conceive only had one "stake in the game" so to speak, it also meant that potentially more women would be vying with one another to advance their only son if royal children were spread across more women rather than concentrated with a few favoured individuals.

---

17 Adams and Fookes, "Queens and Courtesans," 287.

The Power of the Matriarch

This leads us to the final stage in a queen's life, that of matriarch, when she was either literally or ostensibly the head of the family. The importance of royal matriarchs goes right back to the beginnings of monarchy—there is evidence that the king's mother held an identifiable and significant role in the Assyrian, Babylonian, and Elamite courts, where her position may have been superior to that of the king's wife or queen.[18] There has tended to be an assumption that after the death of a husband, a queen faded into the background—packed off to a nunnery or her dowager lands or at least a very much reduced figure at court. This impression has been created by the fact many sources rarely comment on the activities of dowager queens, unless they are the mother of the new ruler and ruling as regent or engaging in activity worthy of scandal or comment, such as Isabella d'Angoulême's decision to remarry after the death of King John of England, start another family in Poitou, and create some political ructions in the French court. As there is great emphasis in chronicles and annals on key milestones in a queen's lifecycle which impact on dynastic history, such as her wedding, coronation, and the birth or death of her children during her years as consort, queens can appear to "drop off the radar" in their dowager years, but that does not mean that her activity and influence at court stopped. Indeed, a woman could reach the peak of her political career during her dowager years as Yolande of Aragon demonstrates—she ably steered the house of Anjou after her husband's death in 1417, acting as regent for her son, pushing forward her family's claims to Aragon, Sicily, Naples, Jerusalem, and Cyprus, setting her daughter up to become queen of France and preparing her granddaughter Margaret to become queen of England. Most significantly however, she played a crucial role in the later stages of the Hundred Years War as a political operator *par excellence* through her role

---

18 Maria Brosius, *Women in Ancient Persia 559–331 BC* (Oxford: Clarendon Press, 1996), 24.

as a trusted advisor and virtual mother to the Dauphin (later Charles VII), helping him to regain his throne and his lands from the English.[19] Like Yolande of Aragon, respect for queen mothers and senior royal women in Southeast Asia appear to have given them an important role to play in affairs of state as well.[20]

It is worth returning to another key difference between the monogamous and polygamous systems—there can only be one king's wife or queen in a monogamous system. In a polygynous court, the king has many wives and women but there is only ever one mother of the ruler—or official one, be it either biological or adopted. Yet a king's mother in a monogamous system may not have necessarily been a queen herself—Cecily Neville, Margaret Beaufort, and Louise of Savoy all provide excellent examples of women from fifteenth and sixteenth-century Europe who had considerable influence as a king's mother when their son came to the throne through less conventional routes. Indeed Louise of Savoy was not only the most powerful woman at the French court during her son François I's reign, she served as regent for him multiple times while he was away on campaign, negotiated his release from captivity after the Battle of Pavia in 1525 and the Peace of the Ladies in 1529 with her former sister-in-law, Margaret of Austria, who represented the interests of her nephew Emperor Charles V. As previously noted, the ruler's mother in a polygynous system was often not the queen, empress, or principal wife—his mother could come from almost any strata within the harem. Thus, while in both systems there is a considerable advantage to being the mother of the heir, it could be argued that there is greater opportunity for uplift for women in a polygamous court. A monogamous queen can

---

19 See Zita Eva Rohr, *Yolande of Aragon (1381–1442), Family and Power: The Reverse of the Tapestry* (New York: Palgrave Macmillan, 2016).

20 Barbara Watson Andaya, *The Flaming Womb: Repositioning Women in Early Modern Southeast Asia* (Honolulu: University of Hawaii Press, 2006), 166.

hope to maintain or even somewhat upgrade her situation by being the mother of the next ruler, but for many women in a harem or inner palace, there is potential opportunity to rise exponentially in rank from being the lowest slave to occupying the place of the queen mother, which in polygynous systems was often the apex of the female court structure.

We can clearly see the power of the queen mother in African monarchies, where she is frequently the most powerful female figure in the realm. Far from being the relic of the last king or a has-been consort, in Africa the queen mother is an "essential ingredient in the nature of royal power and authority."[21] Rather than the king's wife, it is the queen mother who is often the ruler's female "other half" or counterpart, ruling together with distinct but complementary roles. This is reflected in two West African examples—the title for the Akan queen mother, the *ohemmaa*, and the Pabir queen mother, the *maigira*, literally mean "female ruler," not "the king's mother." This role can be filled by the king's actual mother, like the *Iyoba* of Benin. Indeed, in Burundi in East Africa, an heir becomes ineligible for the throne if his own mother dies, as enthronement ceremonies require the installation of a king and his mother. In contrast, in other African monarchies the queen mother may not have been the ruler's biological one, like the aforementioned *maigira* of the Pabir who was a senior daughter of a previous monarch, who was not in the same generation as the king, such as the ruler's aunt. Indeed, in the Oyo and Kotoko societies of Western and Central Africa, the king's biological mother was killed at the time of his accession in order to separate him from his kin group—an extreme form of preventing the queen's family from gaining excessive power from the rise of her son as discussed previously. A similar, but slightly different scenario can be seen in the ritual strangulation of the *Moheofo*, or queen consort/principal wife of the ruler the *Tu'i Tonga* (ruler of Tonga) on

---

21 Ronald Cohen, "Oedipus Rex and Regina: The Queen Mother in Africa," *Africa: Journal of the International African Institute* 47, no. 1 (1977): 14–30 at 14.

her husband's death—thus she too would never be able to wield any power or authority as a queen mother.

The power of royal matriarchs from both monogamous and polygamous societies are clearly visible in three distinct areas: in politics, in managing the dynasty and court and in a sacred role. While the political role of queen mothers will be more fully discussed in the following chapter on rule, it is worth noting here the important role that dowager queens or queen mothers played in royal succession, including the careful management of the succession by the aforementioned Korean queens and the key ritual role played in the enthronement of a new king by the Pabir *maigira*. An even more pivotal role can be seen in the succession practices of the Asante (in modern Ghana), where the *ohemaa*, as the repository of dynastic memory as the "mother of the clan," makes her the ideal person to decide which candidates have the appropriate pedigree for the throne and the wisdom from her senior status gives her the knowledge of who would make a strong ruler. She nominates a new king and consults with elders of the royal family—if they reject her choice, she has two additional opportunities to put forth alternative candidates and even if one of them is selected over her own nominees, her assent is often crucial to any successful accession.[22] Queen mothers could also play a political role in the administrative and bureaucratic element of the realm. In Dahomey, all the queen mothers, or all women who had ever given birth to a king, became "mothers" to key administrative officials, checking on their work and keeping track of their dealings with the king (Cohen, 27).

Managing the court and securing the position of the dynasty was another important area for queen mothers. As matriarchs, royal women were heavily invested in protecting

---

22 Beverly J. Stoeltje, "Creating Chiefs and Queen Mothers in Ghana: Obstacles and Opportunities," in *The Routledge History of Monarchy*, ed. Elena Woodacre, Lucinda H. S. Dean, Chris Jones, Russell E. Martin, and Zita Eva Rohr (London: Routledge, 2019), 569–71.

the future of the dynasty, for the sake of her offspring and descendants. We can see examples from the ancient and classical period which demonstrate the extreme lengths that royal mothers might go to retain their family's power—or their own. In ancient Persia, Artaxerxes II's mother Parysatis was powerful and influential; Artaxerxes "took her advice whenever he needed to protect his throne" (Brosius, 110). Parysatis had those who showed signs of disloyalty to her son killed and may have even killed her son's wife when she showed signs of becoming more influential with the king than his mother. Amestris, the mother of Artaxerxes I was also said to be responsible for deaths at court but played a key role with her daughter Amytis in ending a revolt against her son by Megabyxos, Amytis's husband, and interceding with Artaxerxes to spare his life, ultimately bringing the two men back together. Through her actions, she was able to stabilize a dangerous political situation; Maria Brosius comments (119) that "The king's mother Amestris seemed to know exactly when her support was required, and when she had to intervene for her family." Olympias, the mother of Alexander the Great, was also willing to take decisive, and violent, action to ensure the survival of her family. In the political turbulence that followed the death of her son, Olympias took a considerable risk in throwing her support behind her young grandson, who she had not even met. She successfully faced down those who opposed her—the Macedonian army decided to support the formidable royal matriarch as Alexander's mother and regent for her young grandson. Yet her actions to secure her grandson's place and the dynasty's hold on Macedonia went perhaps too far, triggering a series of deaths including the pretender king Philip III and his wife, as well as the brother of her enemy Cassander and many of his partisans which weakened her popularity and support. Ultimately both Olympias and her grandson were killed as well but her actions show the lengths to with a matriarch could go to protect her family and the future of the dynasty.

In a different political arena, motherhood gave queens the opportunity to move from pawn to player in matrimonial politics as many dynastic matches were coordinated by women—like the *namasole* of Buganda who chose the three most important wives of the king. It is important to note that royal marriages were negotiated not just by dowagers but by consort and regnant queens as well like Maria Theresa of Austria and Victoria of the United Kingdom, who were both important royal matchmakers. However, dowagers could parlay their position as family matriarchs into deep engagement with marriages which would continue the dynasty's survival and success. This may entail diplomatic manoeuvring and extensive correspondence as demonstrated by Mariana of Austria's efforts to secure a bride for her son, Charles II of Spain, or a more physical role in the case of Eleanor of Aquitaine who undertook significant journeys twice to ensure that important matrimonial alliances came to fruition. In 1190, Eleanor travelled from Bordeaux over the Pyrenees to Navarre to complete the negotiations for her son Richard I "the Lionheart" of England's betrothal to the infanta Berengaria and then brought her son's bride to Italy—a formidable journey for a woman who was around seventy years of age at the time. Yet ten years later in 1200, Eleanor crossed the Pyrenees again to ensure the matrimonial success of the family, this time journeying to Castile to select one of her granddaughters, Blanche, to marry the heir to the French throne—bringing another Iberian infanta across the mountains to secure an advantageous marriage. Eleanor proved to be an "indefatigable" matriarch, as Richard of Devizes called her, maintaining her influence and authority into ripe old age, so much so that the wives of her two sons Richard and John, struggled to assert their own position and their rights to queenly lands and revenues, in the shadow of this formidable dowager.

Beyond matrimonial politics, we can also see queen mothers and matriarchs playing important roles in diplomacy, such as the aforementioned Peace of the Ladies negotiated between Louise of Savoy and Margaret of Austria in 1529. Another key diplomatic role played by senior royal women was to serve as intercessors and managers of relationships within the dynasty, harem, and court. As Ruby

Lal has noted, senior women of the Mughal dynasty played an influential role at court, "[...] they counselled Akbar and mediated between dissenting kinsmen. Akbar and other royals sought their advice, and they frequently arbitrated and made suggestions on public matters."[23] One example of this is the part that the dowager Dildar Begum in resolving intradynastic disputes and resolving tension between the Emperor Humayun and his half-brother Hindal, Dildar's son. Dildar counselled her son not to rebel against Humayun and try to proclaim himself king and on another occasion, Dildar went on behalf of Humayun to fetch Hindal and bring him back to the emperor's court so that they could be reconciled.[24] Another example of a royal mother intervening to stop a dispute between her kingly son and his brothers can be found in Hö'elun Eke, mother of Genghis Khan. Hö'elun reputedly bared her breasts to Genghis, reminding her that all of her sons had suckled at her breasts and asked him how he could possibly destroy his brothers, as he looked set to do.[25] Her plea was successful—not only did Genghis mend the rift in the family, he restored his disgraced brother to his former position, and then improved it considerably to make amends. In an equally dramatic fashion, one dowager queen in the Southeast Asian kingdom of Lan Xang once threatened to starve herself to death unless her two sons ended their rivalry (Watson Andaya, 185). Where monarchy is concerned, familial disputes are inherently political, thus a queen's use of her maternal role to end conflict is simultaneously a demonstration of the importance of motherhood and her personal influence on political affairs.

---

23 Ruby Lal, "Mughal Palace Women," in *Servants of the Dynasty*, ed. Walthall, 96–114 at 108.

24 Ruby Lal, *Domesticity and Power in the Early Mughal World* (Cambridge: Cambridge University Press, 2005), 136.

25 Jeannine Davis-Kimball, "Katuns: The Mongolian Queens of the Genghis Khanite," in *Ancient Queens: Archaeological Explorations*, ed. Sarah Milledge Nelson (Walnut Creek: Altamira, 2003), 151–74 at 162.

Queen mothers or dowager queens/empresses could also play a key role in resolving disputes in the harem or inner palace through the effective management and tight control like that exercised by the aforementioned Ottoman *valide* sultans. This was especially vital as the competitive atmosphere of polygynous courts, where women vied to become the ruler's favourite or to protect or promote the claims of their son, could create considerable tension, even violence, when rivals or their offspring were murdered. The infamous Zhao sisters, Zhao Hede and Zhao Feiyan who eventually became empress, rose to prominence in the Chinese court in the first century BCE through a combination of gaining the emperor's favour and ruthlessly eliminating any who stood in their way. Their methods included slander, by which they degraded the position of the virtuous Lady Ban and murder—they were supposedly responsible for the deaths of several of the emperor's offspring by other wives and concubines and were even suspected of murdering Emperor Cheng himself when he died in mysterious circumstances.[26] The Empress Lü dispatched her rival Lady Qi in a particularly brutal manner in 194 BCE, cutting off her hands and feet, putting out her eyes, burning off her ears, and imprisoning her in a latrine, calling her "the Human Pig." This act was considered so heinous by her son, Emperor Xiao Hui, that he suffered from a prolonged period of depression and questioned his own judgement to rule as her son.[27]

Finally, dowagers or queen mothers could play a sacred role, in linking the ruler and royal court to the religious framework or even directly to the divine. For example, Alexander the Great's mother Olympias made offerings to the goddess Hygieia and dedications at the temple of Delphi on his behalf with war booty that he sent back from his eastern campaigns, giving him visibility in important sacred sites during his long

---

26 McMahon, *Women Shall Not Rule*, 76–82.

27 Lisa Raphals, *Sharing the Light: Representation of Women and Virtue in Early China* (Albany: State University of New York Press, 1998), 81–86 and 72.

absence and currying favour with the gods for his continued success. In medieval Europe, some royal widows chose, or were even forced, to go into a nunnery. The ninth-century dowager Holy Roman empress Engelberga joined the convent she herself had founded at Piacenza and Queen Ælfthryth did the same when she retired to Wherwell in Wessex at the end of the tenth century. Yet, adopting a religious life did not necessarily mean a dowager disconnected from politics or life at court as the women of the Hapsburg dynasty demonstrate. Many Hapsburg widows who served as powerful and politically active matriarchs of the dynasty adopted a nun's habit after they were widowed, including Isabella Clara Eugenia and Mariana of Austria. Some women went a step further and moved to a convent after they were widowed, like the Holy Roman Empress Maria who returned to her homeland in Spain and installed herself at the convent of Descalzas Reales, which had a particular link with the royal women of the House of Hapsburg, having been founded in 1559 by Juana of Austria, sister of both Maria and Philip II of Spain. Maria also brought her youngest daughter, Margaret, with her back to Spain and Margaret joined the Poor Clares at Descalzas Reales and became a nun. While ostensibly part of a religious community, Maria and her daughter Margaret (who became known as Margaret of the Cross) wielded considerable influence at court and over Philip III of Spain, who was both Maria's nephew and grandson, given the fact that her brother Philip II had wed Maria's own daughter, Ana—Philip III's mother. In this way they formed a link between court and cloister, as their piety, sanctity, and religious gravitas both demonstrated adherence to ideals of queenly behaviour and gave extra weight to the political counsel they gave.[28] The continuing influence of queenly nuns can also be seen in the case of the two of the wives of Tsar Ivan IV of Russia, Elena Ivanovna Sheremeteva and Anna Alekseevna Koltovskaia. Though both were forced to become nuns by their former husband, they

---

28 See Magdalena S. Sanchez, *The Empress, the Queen and the Nun* (Baltimore: Johns Hopkins Press, 1998).

still retained considerable influence from the convent, working with their former husband's successors after his death to influence donations of land, support for their institutions and for the benefit of their families as dowagers and nuns by leveraging their connection to the Romanovs as former tsaritsas.[29]

While these Christian examples demonstrate the role that dowager queens can play in creating a link between religious establishments and the royal court, queens in other cultural contexts demonstrate a more direct link with the divine. For example, a key part of the position of the *maigira* or Pabir queen mother is to safeguard the sacred objects of the realm which date back to the foundation of the realm itself, reflecting both sacred and political continuity. This gives her a central role in the succession and installation of the king as she "literally legitimatizes the King by providing him with the mystical power of the sacred objects of the state" (Cohen, 23). The queen mothers of the Swazi go one step further—they, and the king, are the only ones in the realm credited with the magical power to make rain.

In conclusion, this chapter has demonstrated the centrality of the family to the lives of queens. Moving from their natal family to their marital one, creating a nuclear family of their own with their spouse and then becoming the female head of the family as a matriarch, the family was the centre of a queen's world and the locus of her power. For consorts particularly, authority stemmed from her familial position: as a representative of her natal family, as the wife or partner of a king, as the mother of heirs and later as the mother (in a biological or virtual sense) of a king. Even for regnant queens, her family was the source of the dynastic pedigree which gave her a claim to the throne, while her marital family could be allies through her husband and she was still under the same pressures to produce heirs as a consort to continue

---

29 See Isolde Thyrêt, "The Royal Women of Ivan IV's Family and the Meaning of Forced Tonsure," in *Servants of the Dynasty*, ed. Walthall, 159–71.

the line. While regnant queens were unlikely to become dowagers, unless they abdicated in favour of their sons as will be discussed in the following chapter, they were still impressive monarchs and matriarchs in their later years, as two eighteenth-century empresses Maria Theresa of Austria and Catherine II of Russia amply demonstrate. In the next chapter, we will explore the ways in which these family connections parlay into co-rulership with fathers, husbands, brothers, and children throughout the lifecycle of a queen.

Chapter 2

Rule

In this chapter we will examine female rulership, looking at practices of corporate monarchy and the ruling partnerships that royal women formed with their natal and marital family members such as parents, siblings, husbands, and children, as well as co-opted virtual family members or favourites. As discussed in the previous chapter, it is family connections which gave a woman the authority to rule, whether her position in her natal family gave her the necessary pedigree to claim the throne, or her partnership with her husband gave her the ability to rule with him, for him, or without him after his death. Maternal links, as a biological or virtual mother, also gave justification for women to play a powerful role as regents and co-rulers. Beyond the family, another key foundation for rule was the queen's affinity, network, or faction. Her affinity was built up of those who were linked to her through bonds of service in her household or as her officials, as well as through personal, familial and political connections. These individuals often owed their position and perquisites to her and thus could offer a fiercely loyal base of support to the queen which enhanced her authority and influence in the court, harem, or inner palace—enabling her to keep or even seize power.

Administration: The Queen's Lands

Rulership entails many elements. A core part of ruling is the control of lands and territories, from the realm itself to the administration of particular lands inherited by or granted to queens and royal women. At the highest level we see queens deeply engaged in the administration of the realm itself as both regnant queens and co-rulers with spouses, family members, and children. Many women had direct and individual control of lands as well which formed part of their office or role. As noted previously, royal sisters and daughters in medieval León ruled a collection of lands and ecclesiastical institutions, collectively known as the *infantazgo*, as *domina* or lady—making them the female equivalent of a lord and an important representative of dynastic authority across the realm and beyond. Queen consorts were customarily given lands upon their marriage which could take the form of a *Morgengabe*, jointure, or dower which was originally intended to provide a secure future for a consort if she was widowed. However, as we can see in the case of English queens, over the course of the high Middle Ages this dower became a means of funding a queen's household, expenses, and patronage during her tenure as consort as well as in her dowager years.[1] Thus a queen's income facilitated the day-to-day functioning of the queen's office and enabled her to maintain a sizeable retinue which played a vital role in projecting the queen's standing and authority. Early modern France offers several examples of queens who increased the size of their household over that of their predecessors and peers to emphasize their power and position, from Anne de Bretagne whose large household signalled her role as both sovereign duchess and queen consort, to Louise of Savoy who sought to underline her role as the king's mother and key advisor and the queen regent Catherine de Medici whose impressive retinue highlighted her position as the most powerful woman in the realm. The queen's lands also enhanced her authority by giving her a considerable domain where she

---

1 See Michele Seah and Katia Wright, "The Medieval English Queen as Landholder: Some Reflections on Sources and Methodology," in *Women and Economic Power in Premodern Royal Courts*, ed. Cathleen Sarti (Leeds: Arc Humanities, 2020), 9–26.

was the effective ruler—for example in medieval Portugal, the queen's lands included six cities where the queen had nearly complete jurisdiction.[2]

Having control of lands was not just an opportunity for queens to demonstrate their administrative abilities through their effective stewardship of her domains, officials, and tenants. It gave the queen financial wherewithal that she could use to pursue her own agenda politically and culturally—as per the old adage "Money is power." As will be discussed in the following chapter, a queen's lands and the wealth derived from them gave her the basis for cultural and political patronage and influence—allowing her to commission artists, construct palaces and religious foundations, and even invest in mills and other enterprises which would further enhance her portfolio. It also gave the queen greater visibility throughout the realm through both her representatives in her lands and her own visits to her dower lands and properties. Her officials and tenants were part of her "affinity" as well, the aforementioned network of people which radiated outwards from her household and court, across the realm and beyond. Henry VIII stripped Catherine of Aragon of her lands when he sought to end his marriage to her—in doing so he aimed to cut both her financial power and break her affinity who might support her cause in the "King's Great Matter," or the royal annulment.[3] Yet this queenly affinity from her control of extensive estates could also work for the king's benefit as well. Laurence Schiller notes (461) that the powerful *namasole* or queen mother of Buganda could use the tenants and officials on her lands

2 Ana Maria S. A. Rodrigues and Manuela Santos Silva, "Private Properties, Seignorial Tributes and Jurisdictional Rents: The Income of the Queens of Portugal in the Late Middle Ages," in *Women and Wealth in Late Medieval Europe*, ed. Theresa Earenfight (New York: Palgrave Macmillan, 2010), 209–28.

3 Michelle Beer, "A Queenly Affinity? Catherine of Aragon's Estates and Henry VIII's Great Matter," *Royal Studies Journal* 6, no. 2 (2019); also published in *Historical Research* 91, no. 253 (2018): 426–45.

as spies for the king or to influence her people to support the king. As in the case of Catherine of Aragon however, a queen's lands could be a means of attacking her—a Bugandan ruler could express his anger at the *namasole* by attacking her lands and damaging her political and financial base.

Many queens were also heiresses with their own lands which they were responsible for administering—from consorts who brought their lands with them into marriages to regnant queens who had inherited the crown themselves. However, while heiresses were very desirable marriage prospects as their territories could expand their husband's realm, queens could often struggle to retain access to their lands and to exercise administrative powers there. Eleanor of Aquitaine was the most desirable heiress of her day given her sizeable and strategic lands in southern France which made her a queen twice over, wedding first Louis VII of France in 1137 and later, after their marriage was annulled in 1152, she wed Henry FitzEmpress, who became Henry II of England. Her Aquitanian lands were so desirable that she had to avoid attempts to kidnap her when she was briefly single after the annulment of her first marriage—one of her potential kidnappers was Henry II's brother, Geoffrey, count of Nantes. These sizeable domains helped to create the Angevin Empire, making her second husband Henry II one of the most powerful men in Europe. Yet Eleanor herself was largely shut out from the administration of her domains as first Louis, then Henry sought to control Aquitaine themselves for their own benefit. However, Eleanor was able to seize the opportunity to return to her lands at certain moments during her long life and take up the reins of administration, for example, ca. 1168 when surviving charters give us evidence of her engagement with the rule of Aquitaine.[4] Her daughter-in-law Isabella d'Angoulême, wife of Eleanor's youngest son John, also struggled to exercise her rights to administer her Angoumois lands while queen consort.

---

4 Marie Hivergneaux, "Aliénor et le Aquitaine: le pouvoir à l'epreuve des chartes (1137–1204)," in *Aliénor d'Aquitaine*, ed. Martin Aurell (Nantes: Editions 303, 2004), 65–70.

Nor did being a regnant queen, or the heiress of an entire kingdom, make the situation for married heiresses any easier with regards to retaining the full administration of their lands. Sticking with the same geographical and temporal context, Juana I of Navarre had her administrative duties for her kingdom largely subsumed by two French kings, first by her father-in-law Philip III during her minority and later by her husband Philip IV during their marriage. Navarre effectively became a French appendage ruled in absentia during this period and the queen remained in Northern France for the majority of her life, possibly never even visiting her own Iberian kingdom. However, there is evidence that she retained some engagement with the administration and defence of the counties of Champagne and Brie which she had also inherited—this was likely facilitated by their greater proximity to the French capital and royal domains.[5] Another royal heiress, Melisende of Jerusalem, also initially struggled to remain engaged with the administration of her domains after her marriage to Fulk of Anjou in 1129. The queen's estrangement from the government of the realm provoked a revolt led by Hugh of Jaffa in 1134, who sought to prevent Fulk from reigning without input from his wife, the rightful heiress, whose right to rule had been repeatedly reinforced by her father Baldwin II.[6]

Succession: Routes to Power

This leads us to the two most important topics in this chapter, routes to power for female rulers and co-rulership with husbands and other family members or co-opted partners. While arguably not as numerous as their male counterparts, it is important to note that examples of regnant queens or female rulers can be found on every continent from the ancient era to the present day—including female pharaohs in ancient

---

5 Woodacre, *Queens Regnant*, 35–43.

6 See Erin Jordan, "Corporate Monarchy in the Twelfth-Century Kingdom of Jerusalem," *Royal Studies Journal* 6, no. 1 (2019): 1–15, especially 6–8.

Egypt, female chiefs in Polynesia, female rulers in Islamic sultanates, and the current host of regnant queens and crown princesses in Europe. Yet women often faced many potential barriers to rulership, from informal ones to legal prohibitions which made it more difficult for female rulers to gain and keep power. The factors which can either prevent a woman from coming to the throne or enhance her chances of rulership can be summarized down to two elements: structural and situational. Structural factors relate to the framework which shapes the context of an heiress's life: the law and/or custom which regulates inheritance and succession as well as the precedent provided by the successful or unsuccessful women who came before her.

Law and custom which explicitly provided for the succession of women, like the *Fueros* of Navarre, greatly facilitated an heiress's path to the throne. It made it possible for her to be formally designated as heir which significantly enhanced her chance of successfully securing the crown—though it did not guarantee she would become queen, as will be discussed shortly in the case of the Empress Matilda. Even the lack of a legal or customary prohibition for female rule could provide an adequate opportunity for a woman to ascend to the throne as it removed legal grounds to prevent her accession. Realms which did not have clear laws, customs, or strong traditions which governed the succession also created an opportunity for women to succeed to the throne. Succession laws or custom which put greater weight on the closest possible blood tie to the previous ruler or an important dynastic predecessor could put a female claimant in a stronger position than a more distantly related male relative. While many European monarchies put greater stress on an agnatic line of descent and developed succession systems which were based on male primogeniture, other dynasties, such as the Bemba and the Akan in Africa, the *Bwij-in-Iroji* or royal line in the Marshall Islands, and several ancient Samoan titles such as the *Tu'i Manu'a* were reckoned solely or frequently via matrilineal descent. Societies with traditions of matrifocality, which placed greater emphasis on matrilineal kinship and the role of mothers as well as a more egalitarian societal framework, could also provide increased opportunities for female rulership.[7] However, it must be noted that women were often considered to be less desirable heirs and were normally second choice to a male relative who had an equal or similarly strong claim.

Often women came to the throne only in the absence, or death, of male heirs and many succession and inheritance laws noted that a woman's claim was only valid in this particular scenario. However, there are rare exceptions where a female heir was given preference or precedence over a male candidate. Examples can be seen in the case of Razia, who was made heir to the Delhi Sultanate in the thirteenth century as her father believed that her rulership abilities were superior to her brothers or when the female Japanese emperor Gemmei abdicated in favour of her daughter, who became Emperor Gensho in 715, rather than the Crown Prince. The precedent of other female rulers also greatly enabled later women who sought to press a claim, although it was often difficult to be the one who started a tradition of regnant queenship. These traditions could be overturned however—for example, Petronilla of Aragon's reign (1137-64) did not prevent the Aragonese from later deciding to bar female claimants from the throne, although succession through the female line was still permissible. Six women ruled Japan as regnant empresses or female emperors between 592 and 770 CE—half of the reigns of this period. In spite of this, and two further female emperors in the seventeenth and eighteenth century, a law was passed in 1889 which prohibited female rule and overturned this precedent. In Southeast Asia, there was an early tradition of legendary regnant queens and even later examples of female monarchs in early modern Patani and Aceh (in modern Malaysia and Indonesia respectively).[8] However this precedent was broken down in part from

---

7 Amirell, "Female Rule," 465-67.

8 Watson Andaya, *The Flaming Womb*, 166-170 and Sher Banu A. L. Khan, *Sovereign Women in a Muslim Kingdom: The Sultanas of Aceh, 1641-1699* (Singapore: NUS Press, 2017).

less supportive traditions in China and Islam, both of which became influential in the region to the extent that at the time of writing, an intensive debate is ongoing over the sultan of Yogyakarta's decision to name the elder of his four daughters as his heir instead of a male relative.[9]

As can be seen in the Japanese situation, one structural factor can overrule another and situational factors can also impede or quash structural factors. Returning to the Empress Matilda, her case was made difficult by a mix of structural and situational factors. She had the benefit of being the officially designated heir by her father Henry I who impelled the nobility of the realm to swear oaths to uphold her claim on his death. However, a lack of precedent was a structural factor which was not in her favour and ultimately a situational factor proved to be crucial—at the time of her father's death in 1135 she was across the Channel and did not immediately travel to England to claim the throne, or possibly could not due to pregnancy related illness. This opened up an opportunity for a rival, her cousin Stephen of Blois, to travel to England and claim the crown for himself. Situational factors can create opportunities for women to rise to power as well, such as the death of a brother, rival claimant, or even husband as will be discussed further shortly.

Moreover, situational factors can lead to the creation of structural ones as the development of the so-called "Salic Law" demonstrates. While it is often assumed, due to later justifications, that the French bar to female succession was an ancient and binding law, the reality is that it came about through an unexpected and hitherto unprecedented situation in Capetian France, the failure of the male line. When Louis X died in 1316 his only living child was his daughter Jeanne— the concern about her taking the throne was not necessarily driven by her sex but the fact that she was extremely young

---

9 There has been extensive media coverage of this debate; for one example see Philip Sherwell, "Java warned of a fresh eruption if its sultan puts his daughter on throne," *The Sunday Times*, World News, March 22, 2020.

and the offspring of a queen, Marguerite of Burgundy, who had been in effect executed for adultery, leaving many to suspect the young princess's legitimacy. However, Louis's second wife, Clémence of Hungary was pregnant, so his brother Philip took the throne temporarily until the child was born. While Clémence did produce the desired son, Jean I the Posthumous, the baby died shortly after birth. Already on the throne, it was not difficult for Philip to stem the protests of those who defended Jeanne's rights as the only child of the last king, and retain the crown himself, becoming Philip V. Yet when Philip died in 1322, he too left only daughters behind— his brother Charles leveraged the precedent that his brother had set and took the crown himself. But in 1328 Charles also died leaving only female surviving issue. At this point the situational factors were incredibly complicated—there were a host of Capetian princesses, all daughters of kings, who had a claim to the throne, and the eldest of them, Isabella, daughter of Philip IV, was Queen of England and the mother of Edward III who could try to claim the French throne via his maternal connection. The only possible answer to prevent an English ruler or civil war between the powerful husbands of the Capetian princesses who sought to put their wife or their children on the throne, was to bar not only female rule but succession through the female line and give the crown to the more distant Valois line. This situation created precedent and custom regarding the succession which became "law" when Richard Lescot used the ancient legislation regarding Salic land in 1358 as a means of retroactively justifying the outcome of the 1328 succession crisis and attempting the block the ongoing English attempt to use Isabella's claim in the Hundred Years War.[10]

While many monarchies utilized systems of dynastic succession, it is important to recognize that some were governed

---

10 See Woodacre, *Queens Regnant*, 51–61 and Derek Whaley, "From a Salic Law to the Salic Law: the creation and re-creation of the royal succession system of medieval France," in *The Routledge History of Monarchy*, ed. Woodacre et al., 443–64.

by principles of election. This did not tend to favour female candidates, yet there are examples of women who were elected as rulers, such as Jadwiga who became the female king of Poland in 1384 and Anna Jagiellon who was elected as the ruler of Poland and Lithuania in 1575. An even more rare type of female succession was via conquest—while some regnant queens such as Isabel I of Castile and Catherine II of Russia expanded their titles and domains militarily, there are a few examples of women like Njinga of Angola who managed to rise to power through conquest in the sixteenth century. A somewhat unorthodox but more common route was for a woman to transition from consort to regnant queen by seizing power, or being invited to assume the throne, after the death of a husband. Returning to the Japanese female emperors, both Kogyoku (r. 642–45, returned as Emperor Samei: r. 655–61) and Jito (r. 690–97) assumed the throne after their Imperial husband's death—the female emperor Gemmei followed her son to the throne in 707.[11] Early modern Russia also has examples of empresses following their husbands to the throne, including Catherine I, who was invited to take the throne after the death of her husband Peter the Great in 1725 and Catherine II, who effectively seized the throne from her husband in a coup in 1762. Shajar al-Durr was also able to take power in thirteenth-century Egypt after the death of her husband Aiyub by concealing his death until she had secured the necessary backing for her own ascent to the throne. Though her reign was short, she was able to achieve two vital criteria of sovereignty for Islamic rulers—the ability to issue coins and having the *khutba* read in her name at Friday prayers (Mernissi, 90).

Yet while many women became rulers, either as the designated heir through dynastic paths of succession or by seizing the opportunity presented by the death of a husband or a political vacuum in the realm, this does not mean that they ruled unopposed. Some female rulers became popular,

11 E. Patricia Tsurumi, "Japan's Early Female Emperors," *Historical Reflections/Réflexions Historiques* 8, no. 1 (1981): 41–49.

even iconic, giving their names to historical eras of peace and prosperity like Elizabeth I of England or Victoria of the United Kingdom. Even though all rulers often face criticism or opposition, a regnant queen's sex provided a vulnerable area to attack her, particularly in patriarchal societies which deemed a woman as a lesser being or "weaker vessel." This can be seen in the intellectual debate about gynocracy in early modern Europe, when writers such as John Knox in his "First Blast of the Trumpet against the Monstrous Regiment of Women" (1558) used biblical justifications to attempt to undermine the rule of women. As rulers who were seen as less desirable than their male counterparts by some, they had to be on guard against potential competitors to the throne and build ruling partnerships with husbands, family members and political allies who could ensure a successful reign.

Co-Rule: Personal and Political Partnership

As discussed at the outset of this volume, all queens were effectively co-rulers and this next section will examine methods and examples of co-rulership with husbands, male relatives, and co-opted partners. For most queens, regnant or consort, co-rulership was often connected to marriage, ruling with their personal as well as political partner. If they were unmarried, like the "Virgin Queen" Elizabeth I of England or Catherine II of Russia who remained unmarried after the death of her husband Peter in 1762, they needed to co-opt partners in rule. These could be purely political partners, like Elizabeth's longstanding and successful collaboration with William Cecil, Lord Burghley, or a more personal connection, such as Catherine's relationship with Potemkin, who shared her ambitions for Russia and served the empress as a general and administrator. Married queens had to negotiate a power sharing dynamic with their husband that both partners were satisfied with—this mutual satisfaction with the distribution of duties and power was more important to their partnership's success than achieving a completely equitable balance. Some male monarchs were happy to let their wife take a dominant role in the partnership due to poor health or disinterest in rule—early modern consorts such as Maria Carolina of Austria, wife of Ferdinand IV of Naples, Marie Clotilde of France, wife of Charles Emmanuel IV of Sardinia, and Nur Jahan, wife of the Mughal Emperor Jahangir are all excellent examples of this scenario.

It must be noted however, that the situation of regnant queens was somewhat different than that of consorts in terms of co-rule. For queens consort, their husband held the sovereign's position and could therefore decide how much of his power and prerogative he wished to share with his wife—if their personal relationship was strong and/or he was willing to cede part or all of his authority to her, it would happen but he was not required, nor necessarily expected, to do so. For women though, as discussed earlier, patriarchal societies expected that a woman would be subject to her husband which made it challenging for the royal couple when the consort was a man and he was in fact, the subject of his wife. There was an expectation that a king consort would either rule for his wife or have considerable power during her reign, which was not the expectation for a female consort. Many regnant queens struggled with husbands who attempted to push them aside and refused to allow them to exercise their rights as sovereign—as discussed earlier, Fulk of Anjou's attempt to cut Melisende of Jerusalem out of governance triggered a revolt to restore the queen's position as rightful heiress and ruler. Husbands who sought to take control of their wife's domains could trigger the breakdown of their marital relationship and even create war in the realm between those who supported the husband or wife—the twelfth-century queens Urraca of León–Castile and Tamar of Georgia both fought bloody conflicts against their husbands but managed to preserve and defend their position. Some queens resorted to extreme lengths to rid themselves of husbands who sought to take power from them and murdered (or were accused of murdering) them, including Giovanna I of Naples, Mary Stuart, Queen of Scots, and Shajar al-Durr in her second marriage. However, an accusation of murdering a consort, however troublesome, could be a queen's undoing—while Giovanna retained her hold on the throne, the death of her first husband Andrew of Hungary brought an invasion from his family who sought to avenge his death. Mary Queen of Scots' enemies used her potential involvement in her husband Darnley's murder to ultimately force her abdication in July 1567 and Shajar al-Durr was arrested by the Mamluks, imprisoned, and then beaten to death for her supposed murder of her second husband Aybek in April 1257.[12]

However, we can see harmonious royal partnerships in scenarios where effective power sharing dynamics were developed between rulers and consorts. The examples of the five reigning queens of Navarre and their male consorts reveal different modes of partnership which can form useful models when evaluating other royal couples. The partnership between Juana I of Navarre and her husband Philip IV can be described as "His Way" as the balance of power firmly favoured both Philip and France. Yet their granddaughter Juana II (the young Jeanne who was the daughter of Louis X overlooked for the French succession in 1316–28) was able to form a different mode of partnership with her husband Philip d'Evreux which could be described as "Team Players." In this style of partnership, Juana II and Philip were able to work together to administer both her Iberian kingdom and his territories in Northern France, even swapping places when needed for the greater benefit of their combined domains. This style of co-rulership was also used by the last regnant queen of Iberian Navarre, Catalina I and her consort, Jean d'Albret. As Catalina's movements were frequently impinged by the fourteen pregnancies she experienced during their marriage, Jean often travelled on her behalf, representing her in various territorial capitals in their domains or undertaking diplomatic missions. A third mode of partnership, "Divide and Conquer," can be seen in the remaining royal pairs: Blanca I and her consort Juan II of Aragon and their daughter Leonor

---

12 David J. Duncan, "Scholarly Views of Shajarat al-Durr: A Need for Consensus," *Arab Studies Quarterly* 22, no. 1 (2000): 51–69 at 53.

and Gaston IV of Foix. In this style, the queen remained in the realm to govern while her consort tended to his own domains. This style can be more cooperative, as in the case of Leonor and Gaston who offered his wife crucial financial and military support from his own territories to help her quell the long term unrest in the kingdom and support her administration—even when physically separate, both husband and wife were consistently working together towards the same political goals. The political interests of Leonor's parents were not so closely aligned however—Juan was frequently in Castile protecting the territory he had inherited and pursuing his own ambitions which at one point created a war between Navarre and Castile that was damaging to his wife's realm.

While harmonious personal partnerships and an effective power sharing dynamic could make a considerable difference in the success of the reign of a female monarch, the importance of a good personal relationship could make an even greater difference to the situation of a consort queen. The degree to which a king desired to share rulership with his consort or even concubine was deeply connected to the strength of their personal relationship. A breakdown in the personal relationship could be disastrous and could lead to consort queens losing their position as well, particularly if she was accused of being unchaste or adulterous. This situation can be seen in the well-known case of Anne Boleyn and also in the aforementioned situations of the French queen Marguerite of Burgundy and the Roman Empress Messalina, the unfaithful wife of the Emperor Claudius. All three of these consorts not only lost their position and their lives but put the position of their children in doubt as well. As noted before the possibility that Marguerite's daughter Jeanne was illegitimate was a factor that made it harder for her to claim the French throne and Anne Boleyn's daughter Elizabeth was declared illegitimate and excluded at various times from the line of succession. Messalina's son, Britannicus's position as imperial heir was damaged by his mother's death and his father's remarriage. He was ultimately supplanted as his father's heir by Claudius's stepson, Nero, and Britannicus's untimely death was likely a move by Nero to permanently eliminate him as a rival for the throne.

In contrast to these disastrous scenarios, a royal couple's strong personal relationship increased a consort's access to the king, particularly intimate access, which gave her more opportunities for influence that could increase her political power within the court and realm. A royal husband was more likely to listen to his wife's opinions or requests if he had affection for her and desired to please her. Yet it is this personal, and indeed sexual, nature of the queen, consort, or concubine's access, which could raise jealousy and concern with others at court and beyond. Criticism of Henrietta Maria, wife of Charles I of England, is an excellent example—Charles's uxorious behaviour led many Protestants to fear that the queen's intimate access and influence would incline him to favour Catholicism. The 1644 pamphlet *The Great Eclipse of the Sun*, expresses this fear of Henrietta Maria's intimate influence:

> [...] hee [Charles] was totally eclipsed by her Counsell, who under the Royall Curtaines, perswaded him to advance the Plots of the Catholikes [...] Ordinary women, can in the Night time perswade their husbands to give them new Gowns [and] Petticotes, and make them grant their desire; and could not Catholick Queen *Mary* (think ye) by her night discourses, encline the King to Popery?[13]

While the impact of "pillow talk" and the queen's ability to effectively influence her husband in intimate or private moments is nearly impossible to quantify or measure, the more public nature of queenly intercession, an important aspect of queenship particularly in medieval Europe, provides more of an opportunity for recorded instances where the queen's wishes were noted as a rationale for the king's

---

13 Anon, *The great eclipse of the sun, or, Charles his waine overclouded, by the evill influences of the moon, the malignancie of ill-aspected planets, and the constellations of retrograde and irregular stares* (London: G.B., 1644), 3.

decisions. Intercession can be seen as a means of co-ruler-ship as king and queen work cooperatively and in a comple-mentary fashion—a king cooperating with the requests and petitions of the queen and the queen complementing the king by offering a counterpart to his role as justiciar and law giver by inclining him to mercy. As Pauline Stafford noted, "Intercession itself is part of the process of power, and could appear so to the petitioner and client."[14] It was also an acceptable method for a queen to engage in the political arena as the mechanism of intercession was linked with bib-lical examples such as the influence of Queen Esther in the Old Testament or the Virgin Mary who was lauded in Catholic Christianity as the ultimate intercessor. This not only fit in with ideals of piety but the expected queenly attributes of peacemaking and diplomacy through seeking mercy and par-dons as well as resolving disputes. A queen's demonstrated ability to successfully intercede with her husband, to incline him to mercy or listen favourably to her petition or one that she championed or put forward to the king, increased her power as courtiers and petitioners sought her assistance and favour. It could even benefit her financially as payments such as the Queen's Gold, a levy of ten percent on all voluntary fines made to the king of England, was designed to recog-nize and recompense the queen for her intercessory abili-ties. Indeed the seventeenth-century writer William Prynne noted in his history of the Queen's Gold that this fine was in recognition of the queen's role as "their future Mediatrix and advocate to the king."[15]

Intercession could have a ceremonial or performative quality, offering the king an opportunity to respond publicly to the queen's request and appear masculine and chivalrous

---

14 Pauline Stafford, *Queen Emma and Queen Edith: Queenship and Women's Power in Eleventh Century England* (Oxford: Blackwell, 1997), 181.

15 William Prynne, *Aurum reginae, or, A compendious tractate and chronological collection of records in the Tower and Court of Exchequer concerning queen-gold* (London: Thomas Ratcliffe, 1668), 5.

rather than weak for changing his mind and granting mercy. Indeed, some accounts of queenly intercession recorded in medieval chronicles can be dramatic, often emphasizing a queen's femininity and role as a dynastic progenitor by describing her as pregnant as in Froissart's famous account of Philippa of Hainault's intercession for the burghers of Calais, or accompanied by young children or both as in the tale of Joan of Navarre's intercession with her first husband Jean IV of Brittany in the Chronicle of St. Denis. However, we have to be careful in our readings of accounts of intercession like these, as chroniclers could dramatize, inflate, or even create scenes of queenly intercession to explain or justify a king's actions. Yet while the representation of these intercessory episodes are not necessarily historically accurate, it still demonstrates a model or understanding of queenly intercession and underlines its importance in the medieval political system.

Co-Rule: Regency and Lieutenancy

A strong personal partnership can not only give a queen consort the ability to influence or intercede with her husband—a royal husband's trust in his wife and belief in her political abilities can lead to opportunities for a queen to co-rule with her husband in a more explicit manner by wielding power on his behalf as a regent or lieutenant. There are a number of scenarios when a king might be unable to rule personally and needed to delegate authority to a representative in what Lachaud and Penman have called "absentee authority" in situations such as interregnum, minority, crusade, captivity, mental illness, and *rex inutilis*.[16] A queen, as the person theoretically closest to the king—his life and ruling partner—could be an ideal choice to become his nom-

---

16 Frédérique Lachaud and Michael Penman, "Introduction: Absentee Authority across Medieval Europe," in *Absentee Authority across Medieval Europe*, ed. Frédérique Lachaud and Michael Penman (Woodbridge: Boydell, 2017), 2.

inated representative, but her gender and the fact that consorts were often foreign could lead to some resistance to their rule on behalf on their husband, or child as will be discussed shortly. In the king's absence, to lead a military campaign, undertake a diplomatic mission or govern other areas of his domain or empire, a queen could be designed as his lieutenant, a term that comes from the Latin *locum tenens*, for a person who occupied the place of someone else.[17] An excellent example of this practice can be seen in Aragon when kings were often absent in order to effectively govern their territory which stretched from the Iberian peninsula all the way to the Aegean at its furthest extent. Here, a lasting precedent for the temporary authority of a queen as the *alter nos* (or "other self") of her husband was established in 1310 by Blanca of Naples who governed while her husband, Jaime II, was on campaign. This tradition continued through the Middle Ages in the effective lieutenancies of queens like Maria de Luna and Maria of Castile and informed the practice of their later Hapsburg successors who used various female members of the dynasty, including wives, aunts, sisters, and daughters as royal representatives to govern regions of their vast empire during the king's absence.

Another scenario in which the king could be "absent" in a completely different sense is during crises of mental or physical health, when they might be unable to rule. The fifteenth century offers a useful comparative example in the scenarios of Isabeau of Bavaria and Margaret of Anjou, two consorts who had to assume greater authority on behalf of husbands who were incapacitated by mental illness. However, while Isabeau's position as the king's stand-in during his periods of incapacity were reinforced by edicts drafted to designate her as his representative and define her authority, Margaret's

---

17 Theresa Earenfight, "Absent Kings: Queens as Political Partners in the Medieval Crown of Aragon," in *Queenship and Political Power in Medieval and Early Modern Spain*, ed. Theresa Earenfight (Aldershot: Ashgate, 2005), 32–52 at 35.

lack of formal appointment gave her opponents leverage to challenge her authority.[18]

While the idea of lieutenancy implies a more temporary notion of "absentee authority," regency offers an alternative model of representative and co-rule. Queenly regency is most strongly associated with rule on behalf of an underaged child until such time as they reach their majority and are able to fully assume the duties of rule. Female regents can be seen in many contexts, from medieval European queens like Maria de Molina and Blanche of Castile to their Islamic counterparts such as Subh of Cordoba and the famous "Sultanate of Women" period in the early modern Ottoman empire as well as across Asia including the regents of the Khitan Liao in China and Mongol khutuns such as Oghul Qaimish. This may entail an extensive period of rule, which could be a challenging period as the realm might be seen as vulnerable to internal trouble and external attack without a strong adult male ruler in charge as seen in the Biblical verse "Woe to thee, O land, when thy king is a child" (Ecclesiasticus 10:16). Again, the queen's authority could be challenged as a woman and often a foreigner—but her authority could be reinforced, as seen previously, by edicts, letters, wills, testaments, or even deathbed wishes of the previous ruler to designate her as regent. A queen could also leverage her familial position, serving as a force for continuity between reigns as the wife of the previous ruler and mother of the next—indeed she could even rule herself as a "ruler stand-in" during a transitional period between the reigns of her husband and son as Ome Tochzin did in Tepechpan between 1507 and 1510 (Boornazian Diel, 265).

---

18 See Rachel Gibbons, "Isabeau de Bavière: reine de France ou "lieutenant-général" du royaume," in *Femmes de pouvoir, femmes politiques durant les derniers siècles du Moyen Âge et au cours de la premiere Renaissance*, ed. Éric Bousmar, Jonathan Dumont, Alain Marchandisse, and Bertrand Schnerb (Brussels: de Boeck, 2012), 101–12 and Helen Maurer, "Un pouvoir à négocier: le cas de Marguerite d'Anjou," in *Femmes de pouvoir*, 113–27.

Queenly regencies were also bolstered by the idea that the mother (or indeed grandmother, aunt, or sister) of a child ruler would naturally have their best interests at heart. A queen could also be seen as a safe choice for the regency—for example in France where Salic Law precluded a woman from ruling in her own right, a female regent could not usurp the authority of a child king in the long term, but an uncle or male relative who had a claim of his own to the throne might be tempted to take the crown in his own right. Indeed after the reign of the first Joseon child king Danjong (r. 1452–55) dissolved into factional chaos between the regency council and ended with the seizure of the throne by the king's uncle, dowager queens were seen as a better choice for the regency and they ruled "behind the bamboo curtain" on behalf of later minority kings (Shin, 116–18). However, while a queenly regency might protect a child ruler from the usurpation of a paternal relative, it could lead to interference from their maternal relatives who might seek to benefit from the regency as can be seen in the case of several scenarios with the families of dowager empresses in Han China. This led to an edict in 222 CE which explicitly barred the empress's family from governmental roles and a general prohibition of the regencies of dowager empresses in 422 when the Liu Song dynasty came to power. Yet female regency returned and ultimately endured for over two millennia until the end of the nineteenth century with the (in)famous regent Empress Dowager Cixi.

While royal mothers were often the logical choice for a female regency, being the direct link between the reigns of their husband and child, women could leverage varied types of relationships with a minority ruler to become their regent. Empresses and ruling women could adopt heirs and promote them to the throne, acting as regents or co-rulers with them as the aforementioned situation of four female rulers of Nayaka in south India in the seventeenth and eighteenth century demonstrates. Sisters and aunts were also logical choices to step into a regency position due to their blood ties to the ruler as well as having the authority of being a dynastic representative themselves. In this way, they could function as key players to stabilize the often difficult transition between reigns, particularly in terms of political crisis or uncertainty in the succession. The example of Sitt al-Mulk in eleventh-century Fatimid Egypt demonstrates this perfectly—she stepped in decisively to settle the issue of the succession after the death of her brother al-Hakim (whom some sources allege she had a hand in murdering), in favour of her nephew al-Zahir. Indeed, she effectively ruled for a critical month before al-Zahir's installation in March 1021, undertaking political purges at court to stem the chaos after her brother's death and ensure her nephew's accession. Sitt remained as regent, or at least remained very influential in the government of the realm by initiating a program of reforms and diplomatic initiatives, until she died two years later in 1023. Other examples of important female regents who were relatives, rather than mothers, include the previously discussed examples of Anne de Beaujeu, regent for her brother Charles VIII of France, and her contemporary Margaret of Austria, regent and later governor of the Low Countries for her nephew Emperor Charles V.

Grandmothers were also logical co-rulers for minority monarchs, particularly when a ruler's mother had predeceased them, following the same principles of blood and maternal duty or affiliation. However, if a mother was still alive, it could be difficult to determine which woman had the greater right to the regency—a mother as the direct parent of the ruler or a grandmother as an experienced elder, who had seniority as the matriarch of the family. After the death of Otto II in 983, Empress Adelheid worked with her daughter-in-law Theophanu to fend off the claims of Duke Henry II of Bavaria to the regency and even to the throne itself. While there appears to have been some rivalry between the two empresses, the long and peaceful regency for Otto III is a testament to their political ability, working with key nobles and churchmen and the other women of the imperial family to ensure stability. This familial cooperation also led to a seamless transition of power between daughter and mother-in-law: Theophanu took the lead in the regency but after her death in 991, Adelheid stepped into the regent's position until 994, when Otto III reached his majority.

Regency was not always uncontested between mother and daughter-in-law—indeed the struggle between them for power could turn deadly. In tenth-century Bohemia, Drahomíra murdered her mother-in-law Ludmila (later St. Ludmila) to gain the regency and the custody of her son Wenceslas I. A similar scenario can be seen in the Ottoman Empire in the seventeenth century. Kösem Sultan was a powerful *valide* sultan who had already wielded considerable power during the reigns of her sons Murad IV and Ibrahim—to the point of deposing and murdering the latter when his behaviour and reign became unstable. When Ibrahim's son Mehmed IV came to the throne in 1648, Kösem faced a threat from his mother Hatice Turhan Sultan and her faction who supported Turhan's right to the regency as Mehmed's mother. Kösem countered by attempting to dethrone Mehmed and replace him with his half-brother Süleyman whose mother Dilasub was less ambitious. In the end, however, the plot was foiled, and it was Kösem who was removed from power, and murdered, most likely at Turhan's direction (Peirce, 252).

As discussed at length in the previous chapter, queen mothers often played a significant role in the governance of the realm even when their children were fully grown as experienced, politically savvy matriarchs and respected elders. They could effectively co-rule with their sons, acting as trusted advisors—indeed Elizabeth Carney notes that "a royal mother remained the person a king could count on most in a world of intrigue and competition."[19] This co-rulership between mother and son could be a formally established tradition as in the "dual monarchy" of Swaziland, where the king and his mother are installed jointly and rule together in all aspects from dealing with legal issues, domestic and international politics to conducting ceremonial, including working rain magic in tandem. Their unity as a

---

19 Elizabeth Donnelly Carney, *Women and Monarchy in Macedonia* (Norman: University of Oklahoma Press, 2000), 32.

ruling pair is remarkable, as Gina Buijs notes "Swazi believe that in all activities the king and queen mother should assist and advise each other, for he is *Inkosi* and she is also *Inkosi*. Together they are spoken of as twins."[20] Louise of Savoy, mother of François I of France, acted as an effective partner in rule to the king as a political counsellor, diplomatic negotiator, and regent or lieutenant during his Italian campaigns as noted previously. Another mother who had a deep and enduring co-rulership with her son was Berenguela of Castile and her son Fernando III in thirteenth-century Iberia. Berenguela was involved in all aspects of government alongside her son, served as regent during his military campaigns and was heavily engaged in diplomacy including negotiations to secure the Leonese throne for her son to reunite León–Castile. Interestingly, Berenguela herself had the inherited the right to the Castilian throne when her brother, Enrique I, died in 1217 but she ceded the throne to her son Fernando almost immediately. Yet she continued to be fully engaged in rule by her son's side, to the extent that she could be seen as a regnant queen—Janna Bianchini has argued that Berenguela's abdication was a tactical move to co-opt her son in rule to give her greater legitimacy and that the two reinforced one another in that "Berenguela's queenship depended as much on Fernando III as his kingship depended on her."[21] Just as in the case of regency, grandmothers could also be important advisors—in a similar fashion to Berenguela, the aforementioned Japanese female emperor Jito abdicated in favour of her grandson Mommu in 697, yet remained a political force at court supporting

20 Gina Buijs, "'Ritual Sisters' or Female Rulers? Gender and Chiefship Revisited in Southern Africa," in *Identity and Networks: Fashioning Gender and Ethnicity across Cultures*, ed. Deborah Fahy Bryceson, Judith Okely, and Jonathan Webber (New York: Berghahn, 2007), 164–78 at 172.

21 Janna Bianchini, *The Queen's Hand: Power and Authority in the Reign of Berenguela of Castile* (Philadelphia: University of Pennsylvania Press, 2012), 178.

Mommu's reign as *dajo tenno* or "great abdicated emperor" until her death in 702.

However, there can also be political and personal tension, even rivalry, between royal mothers and sons. The relationship of Agrippina the Younger and her son, the Roman emperor Nero, is an excellent example of how the relationship between a royal mother and son can deteriorate dramatically and dangerously, once their offspring takes the throne. Agrippina had ruthlessly manoeuvred her son onto the imperial throne—once there Nero recognized the debt he owed to his mother's political acumen and her august lineage which had both made his succession possible. As Nero was in his late teens when he took the throne, Agrippina sought to keep tight control of the young emperor and by extension his government, but this quickly rankled with Nero as he sought to establish himself both as fully grown adult male and as emperor. As Carey Fleiner notes "he could hardly be the father of his country with a nagging mother hanging over him, keeping him a child and undermining his adult authority."[22] Eventually Nero felt that the only way to break free from Agrippina's suffocating influence was to have her murdered in 59 CE.

While the murder of a queen mother at the hands of her offspring was fairly rare, other women were unseated from power in various ways by their sons who did not wish to co-rule with their mothers or continue to do so. Edward III of England was similarly indebted to his mother Isabella of France's manoeuvring to dethrone her husband Edward II and place her son on the throne in 1327. While Isabella enjoyed significant power in the early years of the reign as regent for Edward III, in 1330 her son removed her and her favourite (or according to some sources her lover) Roger Mortimer from power, seizing her lands and removing her from the court. When a woman had her own claim to the throne,

22 Carey Fleiner, "Optima Mater: Power, Influence and the Maternal Bonds between Agrippina the Younger (AD 15–59) and Nero, Emperor of Rome (AD 54–68)," in Woodacre and Fleiner, ed., *Royal Mothers*, 163.

mother and son could be genuine rivals for power. As discussed previously, Melisende of Jerusalem was the heiress of her father Baldwin II and successfully defended her rights with the support of the barony during her marriage to Fulk of Anjou, eventually co-ruling effectively together. After Fulk's death in 1143, she then co-ruled with her son Baldwin III. However, while Baldwin appears to have viewed his mother as a regent who was merely ruling temporarily until he came of age, Melisende clearly felt she was continuing her reign as the rightful heiress with her son, instead of her husband, as her co-ruler. Tension between mother and son regarding her continued rule erupted into civil war in the Crusader States with factions forming around Melisende and Baldwin—eventually by 1152, Baldwin emerged supreme and Melisende was forced to content herself with the governance of the town of Nablus and a far smaller role in the realm at large.

Nor was Melisende the only regnant queen who was pushed aside in favour of her son—in 1567 Mary Queen of Scots was forced to abdicate in favour of her infant son, who became James VI of Scotland and later James I of England as well. The case of Juana I of Castile, often called "la Loca" due to the perception that she was mentally unstable, offers another interesting scenario between royal mother and son. Juana had struggled with co-rulership after her accession to the Castilian throne in 1504 as first her husband, Philip the Fair of Flanders, and then her father, Ferdinand II of Aragon, had sought to effectively rule for her instead of jointly with her, citing her instability as a rationale. In 1516, Ferdinand died and Juana's son Charles came to Iberia to claim his rights in Aragon and his position as co-ruler of Castile with his mother, becoming the third of Juana's male relatives to rule for her, rather than with her. Juana retained the title of Queen of Castile until her death in 1555 but was completely marginalized during her long reign—whether she was not able or not allowed to co-rule is unclear.

Yet there are examples of queens who emerged supreme from co-rulership struggles with their sons—even cases where mothers usurped the rightful place of their sons to take the throne, as can be seen in the cases of the empresses Wu Zetian of China and Irene of Byzantium. Wu Zetian was a savvy political operator who had risen to prominence first as the concubine of the Emperor Taizong and then controversially became empress to his son, Gaozong. Wu continued her power into the reigns of her sons, first ruling for Li Xian but later replaced him with his younger and more compliant brother Li Dan. In 690 CE, Wu moved from being co-ruler to sole ruler, seizing the throne herself to become China's only empress regnant and held onto power until early 705 when plotters took advantage of the empress's long illness to enact a coup which deposed Wu and restored her elder son Li Xian to the throne. The Byzantine empress Irene also began as a regent and co-ruler with her son Constantine VI when he assumed the throne as a ten-year-old in 780, but when Constantine grew older, he sought to rule independently, like Nero and Baldwin III, and plotted to remove her from power, exiling her from court in 790. Irene was able to resume her role as co-ruler with Constantine by 792 but clearly their ruling partnership was damaged as was trust between mother and son. Irene eventually countered with a conspiracy of her own in 797 which resulted in the blinding of Constantine and his removal—Irene was then able to make herself emperor and rule without him until she, like Wu Zetian, was eventually deposed by another palace coup in 802 and exiled to the island of Lesbos.

Co-Rule: Parents and Siblings

Women can also co-rule with their fathers, in a number of different ways. Daughters could be explicit co-rulers with their father as heirs apparent, working alongside their fathers as a means of training them in rulership. Tamar of Georgia's position as her father's heir and co-ruler was formalized when she crowned during his lifetime—a means of anticipatory association practised in other monarchies including the Roman and Byzantine empires, Capetian France and Muscovy. She co-ruled with her father for six years until his death in 1184 and her years as her father's partner in rule arguably solidified her own somewhat precarious position as regnant queen.[23]

Daughters could be engaged in intimate forms of co-rule with their fathers as the situation of Meritaten, who became the "Great Royal Wife" of her father, the controversial Egyptian pharaoh Akenaten, eventually appearing to take over the place of her mother Nefertiri as the first lady of the court. The Mughal princess Jahanara effectively became her father Shah Jahan's ruling partner after the death of her mother Mumtaz Mahal, for whom the famous Taj Mahal was built as a lasting memorial. While not becoming a wife in the manner of Meritaten, Jahanara took her mother's place as Padshah Begum, running the imperial household and harem and entrusted with the keeping of the imperial seal. She was deeply involved in major projects across the empire such as the development of her father's new capital Shahjahanabad and had considerable revenues of thirty lakh rupees (1.5 billion rupees in modern values) to manage and invest in patronage and trade.[24] She also took on familial aspects of her mother's role in terms of guiding her siblings, arranging marriages for them, and attempting to keep peace within the dynasty—an increasingly difficult task. Ultimately, a succession struggle broke out amongst her brothers, leading to the defeat in 1658 of her favourite sibling Dara Shikoh and the imprisonment of Shah Jahan at the hands of her younger brother Aurangzeb. Jahanara remained by her father's side during his incarceration at Agra Fort until he died in 1666, whereupon Aurangzeb invited her back to Delhi to retake the position of Padshah Begum (from her sister Roshanara who had been Aurangzeb's supporter in the civil war), and Jahanara continued as a co-ruler with her sibling instead of her father.

---

23 Lois Huneycutt, "Tamar of Georgia (1184–1213) and the Language of Female Power," in *A Companion to Global Queenship*, ed. Woodacre, 27–38 at 30.

24 Ira Mukhoty, *Daughters of the Sun: Empresses, Queens and Begums of the Mughal Empire* (New Delhi: Aleph, 2018), 169.

A similar scenario can be seen in the case of Jahanara's near contemporary, the Safavid princess Pari Khan Khanum. Pari was a close and trusted advisor of her father Shah Tahmasp, effectively co-ruling with him as a "power behind the throne" and her political abilities and cultural patronage made her a well-respected figure at court. However, while Jahanara ultimately survived an intense succession struggle at the Mughal court, Pari became a victim of the political chaos triggered by the death of her father in 1576. Pari favoured the claim of one of her brothers, Isma'il Mirza over another, Haydar Mirza. She undermined Haydar's plan for the accession by presenting the palace keys to Isma`il's supporters, who then murdered Haydar, who had attempted to disguise himself as a woman in order to escape the palace. As Isma'il had a considerable journey to the capital to claim the throne, Pari ruled in his absence, working to calm the situation at court and in the capital as well as preparing for the new monarch's arrival and installation. Unfortunately, Isma'il's reign proved short, depicted as a "reign of terror"—he did not appear to co-opt his sister Pari in rule and when he died, some sources claim that she was behind his death for cutting her out of power.[25] After this death, Pari appears to have been asked to take the throne herself but declined, citing the stronger claim of her elder brother Muhammad Mirza. When Muhammad took the throne, he showed no inclination to allow Pari to continue as a familial co-ruler or advisor—he may have seen her and her powerful maternal uncle Shamkhal Khan as a threat, as ultimately both were killed at the shah's command in 1578.

The situations of Jahanara and Pari Khan Khanum reveal both the possibilities for co-rulership with fathers and the dangers of becoming embroiled in dynastic disputes with one's siblings. While Jahanara's experience as her father's co-ruler made her useful for her brother Aurengzeb to re-instate as Padshah Begum, Pari's abilities and influence were rejected by her brothers who did not value her counsel as

25 Shohreh Gholsorkhi, "Pari Khan Khanum: A Masterful Safavid Princess," *Iranian Studies* 28, nos. 3–4 (1995), 143–56 at 151–53.

her father had. The intensity of royal siblings' dispute can be magnified when both brothers and sisters have a right to the throne and are expected to explicitly co-rule as partners as in the case of the Ptolemaic dynasty of Egypt. The final generation of this ruling family are a case in point with repeated and deadly fights for the succession. First Berenice usurped the throne of their father Ptolemy XII Auletes and took the crown herself, briefly co-ruling with her mother Cleopatra VI Tryphaena (wife and sister to Ptolemy XII) as Berenice IV before her father returned and had her executed in 55 BCE. After Ptolemy XII died in 51, his children Ptolemy XIII and Cleopatra VII came to the throne but proved to be poor ruling partnership—Julius Caesar ultimately intervened in their squabbles in Cleopatra's favour. Ptolemy XIII, clearly frustrated by Caesar's decision, joined his younger siblings Arsinoë IV and Ptolemy XIV who were set to rule Cyprus as another ruling brother–sister pair and the three became a united front and a focal point for resistance to both their sister Cleopatra's rule and Roman interference in Egypt. This resistance was broken by Ptolemy's death in the Battle of the Nile in 47 BCE and Arsinoë was taken captive and appeared in Caesar's triumph in Rome the following year. The youngest brother, Ptolemy XIV was made his sister Cleopatra's co-ruler to satisfy the norms of Ptolemaic sibling rule, but died in 44 BCE, possibly on the orders of his sister-queen who was finally a sole ruler, free of brother and sister rivals.

Yet, royal women could co-rule with their siblings in harmony, with elder sisters serving as capable regents as seen in the earlier example of Anne de Beaujeu and Charles VIII of France. An additional case is Pulcheria who served as regent of the Eastern Roman Empire for her brother Theodosius II in the fifth century—remaining influential in his court after his majority until he married and his wife Eudocia and her supporters diminished Pulcheria's power and influence. Co-rule between brothers and sisters worked best when structures of rank were well defined, the role of all siblings was clear and custom reinforced respect and honour between siblings, as in the case of Tonga where "the brother was obliged to support the sister, and the descendants of a brother were obliged to support the descendants of the sister."[26] While the ruler, the *Tu'i Tonga*, is customarily male, his sister, the *Tu'i Tonga Fefine* (the female *Tu'i Tonga*), technically outranked him and all of his descendants and commanded great respect due to her divine powers, sacred status, and exalted position in society. The idea of sibling co-rulership, with each having a powerful and complementary role, is reinforced by the Tongan cultural custom of brothers and sisters jointly leading familial groups or *kainga*, again with both siblings having clearly defined corresponding areas of authority. Sisters can also share facets of rule with their brothers—for example in Uganda the kingdoms of Bunyoro–Kitara and Busongora–Chewzi both use the title of *kalyota*, or the king's "official sister." The *kalyota*, who could be a full or half sibling, could be viewed as a female counterpart of her sovereign brother with considerable authority in terms of hearing and resolving disputes and issues of precedence and administered sizeable estates of her own (Buijs, 165).

This chapter has explored many different facets of rulership, from the varied roles and responsibilities of the queen's office, examining different routes to power including formalized succession to political opportunities and even conquest. It has also discussed the variety of ways in which women could co-rule with spouses, siblings, children, family members, and favourites. Understanding the importance of family relationships, marital partnerships, and dynastic mechanisms for rule as discussed in the previous chapter has informed our understanding of the way in which women co-ruled by leveraging the value of their dynastic lineage and connections, hereditary rights and familial bonds. Ultimately, this chapter has shown the deep political engagement of royal women in both explicit roles and public demonstrations of authority as well as their significant influence through their intimate relationships and family ties which could be an equally important, though more difficult to evidence, mode of exercising power.

---

26 Elizabeth Wood Ellem, "Queen Salote Tupou of Tonga as Tu'i Fefine," *Journal of Pacific History* 22, no. 4 (1987): 209–27 at 210.

Chapter 3

Image

For a queen, image was everything. As the most visible woman In the realm—even if she was cloistered or behind a screen, her presence was still felt at court and by her subjects—a queen's ability to craft a positive image was not only crucial for her own reputation but for the effective functioning of the monarchy as a whole. If her image crafting was successful, it would serve her well not only in life, but in the afterlife by creating a positive legacy which would ensure for centuries or even millennia. If she got it wrong, it could have a catastrophic impact which could lead to the loss of her position or even the downfall of the monarchy as well as a "black legend" which could persist in popular memory and culture like Wu Zetian, Catherine de Medici, and Marie Antoinette.

Image fashioning spoke directly to the ideals of queenship, as queens sought to create an image which reflected these expectations to demonstrate her successful exercise of the queen's office. By creating an image which reflected contemporary understandings of queenly virtues she simultaneously reinforced these ideals and created a model for future queens to follow and emulate—or if her image jarred with ideals of queenly behaviour, she could become an example of an "anti-worthy" whose life would become a salutary lesson for other royal women in what not to do, as discussed in the introduction. This chapter will discuss how royal women developed and projected an image which resonated with these queenly virtues through acts of patronage, dress, and display and by performing rituals and ceremony. It will demonstrate the deep connections between patronage, display, and ceremonial both as a means of image creation and as central aspects of queenly activity as well as highlight continuous links between these three elements and the wider context of religion, culture, and power.

Patronage

As discussed in the opening chapter, patronage has long attracted considerable attention from scholars as a central facet of queenship. This section will examine the many forms of patronage which are intertwined and multi-faceted including various aspects of religious, cultural, and educational patronage. There is a political element to consider as well—as noted previously, a key means of political patronage was the queen's ability to procure appointments both within her household and affinity—and to provide those within her network opportunities for advancement and financial benefits. We have also discussed the queen's influence and intercession as a means of political patronage—enabling her to assist others to improve their position or to alleviate the king's disfavour or punishments. This chapter will consider the political benefits of other forms of patronage, evaluating how cultural commissions and the support of religious and educational institutions could secure and enhance her position and authority. This chapter will also reinforce the vital importance of the queen's finances—without adequate revenue, salary, or funds, her ability to engage in any form of patronage was hampered which in turn could weaken her position and her ability to craft both a positive image and an enduring legacy.

Earlier discussions of queenly ideals and activity revealed a shared emphasis on piety across all religions and cultures in the premodern world which queens were expected to exemplify. An effective way for a royal woman to visibly demonstrate this virtue, and leave a legacy of being a pious queen, was to engage in religious patronage and other aspects of performative piety. Religious patronage arguably connects with nearly every form and aspect of patronage in some way which makes it the perfect place to begin our discussion. For example, if a queen sponsors the foundation of a new religious building, she is engaging in both religious and architectural patronage—if we include the decoration of the building or perhaps the commission of her tomb inside it, we are looking at aspects of artistic and cultural patronage as well. Given how deeply religion and power—or religion and monarchy—are connected, religious patronage is arguably highly political as well.

Religious patronage has similarities with political patronage as well—in this case a queen is using her influence and position to support religious figures, by giving them an entrée to court, funds, and/or a place in her retinue which increases the visibility of these religious figures and the reach of their faith across the realm. Indeed, many queens are linked with conversion narratives or credited with bringing religious change to their realm through their sponsorship of particular religious figures and their faiths. An example from fifth-century Europe is Clotilde, the wife of Clovis I, king of the Franks. While Clotilde was a Christian, her husband was a pagan—initially he resisted adopting her faith but eventually Clovis converted in 496, when he secured a victory in battle after promising to adopt Christianity if he won. Thus, Clotilde, through her influence on her husband, played a crucial role in the conversion of the Frankish kingdom. Her legacy as a pious queen was further enhanced by extensive religious patronage—ultimately one of her sons became a saint (St. Cloud) and she was eventually canonized herself. In Asia, many royal women were credited with being vital to the spread of Buddhism in royal courts and beyond. In Dai Viet or modern Vietnam in the eleventh century, the queen mother, Phu Thanh Cam Linh Nhan's interest in Buddhism led her to invite monks for a feast so she could ask them about their faith. A contemporary chronicle notes:

> The queen mother was very happy with Thong Bien's reply, so she honoured him with the title Monk Scribe [Tang Luc] and gave him a purple robe. She gave him the sobriquet

Thong Bien Quoc Su, which means "National Preceptor with Consummate Elegance" and rewarded him munificently.[1]

This queen mother, through her interest in Buddhism, played a central role in cementing its presence in Vietnam—many courtiers and subjects followed her lead and her support greatly increased Buddhism's reach across the realm.

Having the support of religious figures and institutions could cement or support the queen's position which could be vitally important in times of crisis—for example Pope Nicolas I's support for Queen Theutberga was crucial when Lothar II of Lotharingia sought to divorce her in the ninth century. Religious patronage could be a way to gain political alliances and support in a secular context as well. Xia (or Tangut) empresses dowager used the patronage of Buddhism to reinforce their rule as regents in the late eleventh century as it allowed them "to cultivate a wide range of allies across clan lines and outside the military elite. Through her Buddhist activities and Sangha allies, the empress dowager expressed personal piety, gained support for her rule [...] and defended the throne."[2] Wu Zetian also used religious patronage to secure her position as first a regent and then regnant empress and "convince her people that she had the right to rule."[3] Wu's commissions include the spectacular giant statues of the Buddha and Bodhisattvas at the Longmen Grottoes—the statue of the buddha Vairocana has been viewed by some as a portrait of the empress herself. Wu built on these associations with the Buddha by adding the name of the Bodhisattva Maitreya to her titles to divinely enhance her authority.

---

1 "The Queen Mother and Thong Bien (Excerpt from *Eminent Monks of the Thien Community* [1337])," in *Sources of Vietnamese Tradition*, ed. George E. Dutton, Jayne S. Werner, and John K. Whitemore (New York: Columbia University Press, 2012), 48–51 at 50.

2 Ruth W. Dunnell, *The Great State of White and High: Buddhism and State Formation in Eleventh-Century Xia* (Honolulu: University of Hawaii Press, 1996), 51.

3 Elisabetta Colla, "When the Emperor is a Woman: The Case of Wu Zetian (624–705), 'The Emulator of Heaven'," in *A Companion to Global Queenship*, ed. Woodacre, 13–25 at 20.

Another form of religious patronage which enhanced reputation of royal women both in life and after death was the foundation or amelioration of religious institutions, including shrines, temples, churches, monastic institutions, and religious educational facilities. An example from medieval Iberia is Isabel of Aragon, queen of Portugal, who patronized hospitals, monastic foundations, and churches across Portugal in the fourteenth century. As a widow, Isabel moved to a palace she built adjacent to the monastery she had founded at Santa Clara-a-Velha to personally supervise the construction of the convent and its hospital on site. The queen's zeal for religious construction amplified her reputation as a pious queen, leading to her ultimate canonization as St. Elizabeth of Portugal. In addition to demonstrating power and piety, religious architectural patronage could also highlight dynastic allegiance and familial connections. The development of Greyfriars in London links the patronage of three successive English queens in the fourteenth century—Margaret of France began a program of construction there in 1306 which was continued by her relatives Isabella of France and Philippa of Hainault. For all three women, the development of Greyfriars was not just a means of asserting their queenly power, wealth, and piety through their support of the institution but a means to reinforce their mutual Capetian connections by continuing a dynastic tradition of patronizing the Franciscan order.

Wider connections can also be displayed in different ways through architectural religious patronage—the ability of royal women in the Ottoman and Timrud empires to patronize the construction of mosques such as the Yeni Valide Mosque complex in Istanbul built by Safiye Sultan and Hatice Turhan Sultan or Gawhar Shad's construction of two prominent Friday mosques in Mashhad and Herat, derived from traditions in their shared Turco-Mongol heritage.[4] Founding a major reli-

---

4 Nushin Arbabzadah, "Women and Religious Patronage in the Timrud Empire," in *Afghanistan's Islam: From Conversion to the Taliban*, ed. Nile Green (Berkeley: University of California Press, 2017), 60.

gious building could create a long lasting legacy for a royal woman as the building was used continuously for generations or even centuries, ensuring that her name and pious reputation endured. Royal and elite Muslim women were encouraged to take part in the architectural patronage of *waqf* or endowed religious institutions such as mosques, khanqahs (a place for religious meetings and retreats), soup kitchens, mausoleums, and madrasas (institutes of religious education). European queens were also keen patrons of education who founded and developed colleges and universities. Juana I of Navarre left an endowment in her will and extensive instructions for the foundation of the Collège de Navarre in Paris—her statue commemorating her role as the college's patron, holding a miniature version of the building in her arms, can still be seen in the Bode Museum in Berlin today. In England, the universities of Oxford and Cambridge benefitted from the patronage of queens. Oxford's Queen's College was founded in 1341 by Philippa of Hainault's clerk Robert Eglesfield who named her as its patroness so the college could benefit from her support. Queens' College, Cambridge was patronized by several English queens from Margaret of Anjou and Elizabeth Woodville who are both credited as initial foundresses up to modern queens Elizabeth Bowes-Lyon and her daughter Elizabeth II.

Royal women commissioned a range of buildings which left a clear mark on both urban and rural landscapes including markets, hospitals, caravanserai, and palaces. Palaces and gardens were built in Paris by three early modern French queens: Catherine de Medici's Tuileries, Marguerite de Valois's on the opposite bank of the Seine in the faubourg Saint-Germain and Marie de Medici's Palais Médicis (now known as the Palais de Luxembourg) all provided an impetus for the city to push its development westwards.[5] Queens could also play a major role in the (re)development of palaces through architectural patronage. The late seventeenth century offers two excellent examples in Mary II of England who played a vital

---

5 William O. Goode, "Moving West: Three French Queens and the Urban History of Paris," *The French Review* 73, no. 6 (2000): 1116–29.

role in reshaping both Hampton Court Palace and Kensington Palace and in Hedwig Eleonora, Queen of Sweden, who played a major role in the construction and redevelopment of several palaces including Ulriksdal, Karlberg, Strömsholm, and Drottingholm.

Royal palaces could also function as repositories for the collections of queens which demonstrated their wealth, status, taste, personal interests, and dynastic identity. Examples include the Hermitage in St. Petersburg—Catherine the Great's famous showpiece for her extensive art collection or the Swedish queen Louisa Ulrika's collection at Drottingholm which featured antiquities, coins, medals, minerals, shells, corals, as well as paintings and literary works. Another eighteenth-century queen who possessed an impressive literary collection was Caroline of Ansbach who commissioned a new royal library to house it at St. James' Palace. The collections of queens also facilitated cultural transfer and exchange between courts and across religious and political boundaries through gift-exchange, bequests, and commissions.

Central Europe offers many examples of royal women as cultural conduits through patronage and the collections that they brought with them from their natal to marital homes. Byzantine brides such as the Holy Roman empress Theophanu, Anna, wife of the Kievan Rus' prince Vladimir Sviatoslavich, and Zoe (Sofia) Palaeologus, wife of Ivan III, Grand Prince of Moscow all brought cultural influence to their marital courts through the objects and artisans they brought with them when they married. In the sixteenth century, the Italian princess Bona Sforza had a significant cultural impact on the Polish–Lithuanian court. Bona's marriage to Zygmunt I increased the influence from the Italian Renaissance in art, architecture, clothing, and even fine dining. Bona and Zygmunt created a cultured and cosmopolitan court which had a profound influence on their children—their daughters Katarzyna, queen of Sweden, and Zofia, duchess of Braunschweig-Wolfenbüttel, became important cultural patrons and collectors, using their dynastic contacts to enhance their collections and to recommend artists, artisans, writers to one another, all of which were significant factors in cultural exchange.[6]

Cultural patronage offered queens an excellent opportunity for influence by importing personnel and fashions from their homelands, raising the profile of particular artists and writers and creating opportunities and venues for creative activities and works to flourish. Two queens of Italian origin brought artists and art forms from their native lands: Catherine de Medici's sponsorship of ballets established this form of dance at the French court and Mary of Modena's patronage of Italian musicians like Innocenzo Fede who served her as Master of Music introduced Italian musical styles to the English court. Queens could go beyond patronage to participate in cultural creations themselves as Anna of Denmark did as both a sponsor of and performer in masques at the Jacobean court. Queens could also use the funds at their disposal to commission new works which had both cultural and societal significance. For example, in the late eighteenth century the "matronage" of queens such Charlotte of Mecklenburg-Strelitz, queen of England, to commission works from women such as Angelica Kaufmann, Catherine Read, and others greatly enhanced the status of female artists.[7]

Some of the commissions given to these female artists were portraits—Elisabeth Vigée le Brun painted over six hundred portraits during her long career, including thirty of Marie Antoinette. Her memoirs recount her experience of painting not only at the French court but working for other contemporary queens such as Maria Carolina of Naples and Catherine II of Russia. Portraits were perhaps the ultimate element of patronage for image creation, and like other

---

6 Almut Bues, "Art Collection as Dynastic Tools: The Jagiellonian Princesses Kataryzna, Queen of Sweden and Zofia, Duchess of Braunschweig-Wolfenbüttel," in *Queens Consort, Cultural Transfer and European Politics, c. 1500–1800*, ed. Helen Watanabe O'Kelly and Adam Morton (London: Routledge, 2017), 15–36.

7 Heidi A. Strobel, "Royal 'Matronage' of Women Artists in the late 18th Century," *Woman's Art Journal* 26, no. 2 (2005–6): 3–9.

forms of patronage discussed previously, they could carry political messages to bolster a queen's position as well. Marie de Medici, as queen regent of France in the seventeenth century, commissioned an epic cycle of twenty-four paintings which traced her rise from Italian princess to consort of Henri IV and then regent for Louis XIII from the renowned artist Peter Paul Rubens. These paintings were designed to hang in the aforementioned palace which she built as her new residence in Paris—combining her architectural and cultural patronage to send a strong message about her wealth, power and influence. A different type of portrait which also demonstrates the power of a royal mother is the depiction of Agrippina the Younger on a relief from the Sebasteion al Aphrodias where she is pictured crowning her son, Emperor Nero. While the scene was figurative rather than a depiction of his actual coronation, Elizabeth Bartman notes that "the Sebasteion relief is overt in its message of womb as kingmaker."[8]

Portraits can also reflect queenly ideals, or represent queens in an idealized form—for example as a personification of beauty and mirrors of contemporary fashions as can be seen in the early eighth-century stucco portrait of Lady K'abal Xook, Queen of Yaxchilian, which "epitomizes Maya conceptions of feminine beauty."[9] Franz Xaver Winterhalter's famous portraits of the nineteenth-century queens Victoria of the United Kingdom, Empress Eugenie of France, and Empress Elisabeth of Austria (also known as Sisi or Sissi) idealized and celebrated their looks the world over. Indeed, Empress Sisi was so conscious of the reception and consumption of her beautiful image by the general public that she became obsessed with the maintenance of her long chestnut

---

8 Elizabeth Bartman, "Early Imperial Female Portraiture," in *A Companion to Women in the Ancient World*, ed. Sharon L. James and Sheila Dillon (Chichester: Wiley-Blackwell, 2012), 414–22 at 419.

9 Andrew D. Turner and Michael D. Coe, "A Portrait of Lady K'abal Xook, Queen of Yaxchilan," *Yale University Art Bulletin* (2018), 66–73 at 67.

locks, keeping her figure slim and fending off the ravages of aging with unusual creams and treatments.

In addition to displaying ideals of feminine beauty, queenly portraits can also reinforce the ideal of the pious queen by representing them as holy or even quasi-divine. The portraits of queens in the illuminated twelfth-century cartulary the *Liber testamentorum* features portraits of royal women with haloes, which recognizes their "spiritual guardianship of royal families, responsible for praying for the souls of the deceased, and patronising monasteries to ensure the perpetuation of prayer and the preservation of memory."[10] A cameo portrait of Livia, wife of the Roman emperor Augustus, portrays her as both goddess, linking her with Cybele, Ceres, and Venus, and priestess, by the bust of her husband she holds which symbolizes her role as the first priestess of the Imperial cult after Augustus's death.

Display

While portraiture can be seen as a form of patronage, at least in regard to the portraits a queen commissioned, it is also closely linked to display. Display is another vital element of image creation which can take many forms from a queen's dress, adornment, and the decoration of her palaces to the objects which she collected in life and distributed as gifts and bequests—or had buried with her—in death. Display is a crucial means of demonstrating majesty and affirming her elevated status, wealth, power, and authority. However, it was crucial to get the balance right between creating a sense of awe in the observer and adhering to expectations of queenly modesty and decorum. Pushing the richness of display too far could lead to criticism of the queen being spendthrift or obsessed with luxury and the superficiality of appearance as

---

10 Shannon L. Wearing, "Holy Donors, Mighty Queens: Imaging Women in the Spanish Cathedral Cartularies of the Long Twelfth Century," *Journal of Medieval History* 42, no. 1 (2016): 76–106 at 89–90.

Marie Antoinette was for her elaborate wigs and plethora of new dresses commissioned each season from her couturière Rose Bertin which featured in her portraits by Vigée le Brun. In contrast, while Queen Alexandra of the United Kingdom also spent considerable sums on clothing, the queen managed to be both regal and approachable which enhanced her popularity with her subjects using "her clothing, judged on the merits of any given event or time of day, to both fit into upper-class Britain and to simultaneously stand out as a prominent public figure."[11]

Dress also could be a powerful tool for queens to assert their personal, national, and dynastic identity as seen in the cases Eleanor of Austria, queen of France, and Eleonora de Toledo, duchess of Florence, who signalled their continued allegiance to their natal dynasty by continuing to wear Iberian clothing and hairstyles. However, this strategy could backfire on queens by emphasizing that they were foreigners—the Spanish princess Maria Teresa and her retinue were mocked by French observers for the *guardainfanta* or farthingales they wore during the ceremonial held to celebrate her impending marriage to Louis XIV in 1660. To avoid this kind of disapprobation royal women could be pressured to adopt the dress of their marital courts, for example the French princess Elisabeth de Bourbon was sent a dress in the Spanish fashion by the Hapsburg archduchess Isabella Clara Eugenia in 1612 to demonstrate how she should dress as Philip III of Spain's queen.

The adornment of the queen's body was a vital means of projecting her status as queen and the authority which came from her tenure of the queen's office. Indeed, many fabrics such as cloth of gold or those dyed with Tyrian purple, were reserved by law to the royal family, thus wearing garments made of these materials instantly reminded viewers of the queen's exalted rank. Clothing could be particularly important for reinforcing her queenly status at a moment when her rank was in transition, during her installation as consort or at

11 Kate Strasdin, *Inside the Royal Wardrobe: A Dress History of Queen Alexandra* (London: Bloomsbury, 2017), 6.

the death of her husband or if it was under threat, for example when Margaret Tudor lost the Scottish regency in 1515 and was living in exile in England. Margaret's brother Henry VIII continued to fund her expensive apparel to assuage his personal and dynastic honour as well as emphasizing her status as Queen of Scots to reassert her right to the regency, which Henry wanted her to reclaim for England's political benefit. Thus, wearing costly fabrics not only demonstrated a queen's own wealth, but her visibility meant that it was a means of projecting her husband's, family's, and by extension the realm's power, financial health, and glory. [12]

Jewellery was another form of adornment and display which was deeply linked to the queen's royal position. Queens not only projected their status through the jewels they wore but they used jewels to reinforce their position by gifting them across their courtly and international networks, which helped to develop their strength and reach. Queens also received jewels as gifts and markers of key moments in their lifecycle, such as their wedding, coronation, and the birth of heirs. These key ceremonial events were also occasions to wear their queenly regalia—pieces which had often been handed down for centuries and were imbued with great significance due to their use in ritual and the vital role of objects such as crowns, orbs, and sceptres as the symbol of monarchical power itself.

As well as jewels, the queen's ceremonial clothing had both deep cultural significance and formed yet another element of display. The queens of Joseon Korea had very specific attire that was worn for different ceremonies following the model of the Chinese "Rites of Zhou" which stipulated which type of robe, headdress, and colours—with their meaningful motifs and colours—were appropriate for specific rituals. Her most important ceremonial robe was the *jeokui* or "pheasant robe" which was worn for major rituals and occasions. The pheasants symbolized both Confucian and queenly ideals—its five colours represented the five virtues of benevolence, justice, courtesy, integrity, and wisdom as well as the five directions and the five elements. By wearing the robe, the queen reinforced these shared cultural values both to her subject and to herself as "the pheasants on the royal robe were to remind the queen to remain a virtuous woman" (Shin, 103).

Ritual and Ceremonial

Ritual and ceremonial underpinned the practice of queenship, the daily rhythm of court life, and even the functioning of monarchy itself. Indeed, in many cultures rituals conducted by royal figures were believed to have an essential role in maintaining harmony between the cosmic order between divine and humanity, ensuring adequate rainfall and good harvests, which could have potentially disastrous impacts if the ceremonies were not performed correctly. Ritual and ceremonial defined and demonstrated the queen's role. Routine rituals at court which the queen led and in which she participated on a daily basis reinforced her position as the preeminent woman in the realm and as a model to her female courtiers and subjects. Major ceremonial events literally marked her entry into her role—from baptism which confirmed her royal status at birth, to her wedding and/or coronation which installed her as the queen to her funeral which reaffirmed her importance during her life and memorialized her role as a (co-)ruler as well as her familial connections to past, present, and future rulers.

Fortunately for scholars of queenship, given the vital importance of ritual and ceremonial to the court and monarchy, this is a particularly well recorded aspect of the queen's role. Surviving manuals from court ordinances and *ordines coronationis* laid out how rituals should be conducted and delineated the queen's role in these events. Precise records were kept of key ceremonies for royal weddings, queenly coronations, civic entries, and the birth of heirs as they were important moments in national and dynastic history. Indeed, for some royal women these records form the best contemporary sources we have for their lives as their central role in these momentous events were noted down. However, these sources have potential issues regarding the reliability of witnesses to events, the agenda of chroniclers which affects how they portray these moments, and how much focus they give to the queen's role in them while *ordines* provide a manual to how ceremonies should take place rather than what actually happened. Yet these records still give us a useful picture of the significance of court ritual and royal ceremonial and an understanding of the place of the queen in these important events.

Ritual and ceremonial take many different forms, from those which follow a predictable cycle from daily ritual to annual observances to those which are infrequent, irregular, or even extraordinary. Daily ritual activities, such as religious services and devotions and rituals connected to rising, going to bed, and dining, affirmed rank and court protocol and the queen's position as the preeminent woman at court as the leader or focus of these ritual activities. For example, the queen's daily religious rituals were magnified by the retinue of courtiers who accompanied her to a church, temple, mosque, or shrine or joined her in prayers within the confines of her apartments or the harem, zenana, or inner palace—this underlined both the significance of the ritual and the importance of the queen by the number or attendants who participated with her.

Indeed, there is a religious element to many court ceremonies—from daily religious observances to the most significant events—which gave the queen an opportunity to engage in performative piety as an exemplar of behaviour to her subjects. This could be demonstrated in countless ways—from attending or sponsoring religious services, participating in significant recurring ceremonies, or undertaking acts of pilgrimage. The latter could be particularly effective in developing a queen's reputation for piety, as in the case of Blanca I of Navarre who frequently went on pilgrimage and once took her entire court with her in 1433 to celebrate the Assumption of the Virgin Mary at Santa María del Pilar in Zaragoza. Another example is the tenth-century Japanese dowager empress Higashisanjo-in, whose frequent pilgrimages to the Buddhist temple at Ishiyamadera were immortalized in a scroll as a model to encourage later donors to follow her pious and illustrious example and patronize the shrine in turn.[13] In some cultures, royal women did more than attend or patronize religious services, they performed them as early Roman empresses did as priestesses of the Imperial cult or as in the case of Mayan royal women who took part in sacrificial rituals. Some royal women were even the focus of religious rituals, as in the case of the Ptolemaic queen Arsinoë II who was worshipped in both Greek and Egyptian temples as a goddess—an entire festival, the Arsinoeia, was created to honour her divinity.

However, not all royal ceremonial was as intensely linked to religion. Progresses and civic entries could be a vital means of articulating the queen's authority and projecting her image to her subjects. Elizabeth I did this masterfully, using her annual progress to reinforce her power as monarch and the image of "Gloriana" across both urban and rural areas of England. Royal women could also play a key role in rituals connected to war and peace. Indeed, some queens took part in battle themselves as formidable warriors such as Teri'itaria of Huahine, consort of the early nineteenth-century chief Pomare II of Tahiti, who was so impressive in warfare that she was believed to be an incarnation of the war goddess Toimata.[14] Maya queens were engaged in both warfare itself and performed rituals which supported it, such as one which called on their ancestors to help them be victorious in

---

13 Elizabeth Morrissey, "Retired Empress and Buddhist Patron: Higashisanjo-in Donates a Set of Icon Curtains in the *Illustrated Legends of Ishiyamadera*," in *Women, Rites and Ritual Objects in Premodern Japan*, ed. Karen M. Gerhart (Leiden: Brill, 2018), 343–68.

14 Niel Gunson, "Sacred Women Chiefs and Female 'Headmen' in Polynesian History," *The Journal of Pacific History* 22, no. 3 (1987): 139–72 at 143.

battle. [15] In Buganda, chiefs selected particular royal wives to accompany him on campaigns—their role included guarding the war gods and performing rituals as well as more supportive tasks such as cooking, sharpening spears and attending to the wounded.[16] Women could also play a key ritual role in war and peace though ceremonial to celebrate key victories; for example Joan of Navarre led a procession from St. Paul's to Westminster in 1415, where a mass of thanksgiving was held for Henry V's victory at Agincourt and offerings where given at the shrine of Edward the Confessor. Given the vital role that ambassadors and envoys played in peacemaking and diplomacy as representatives of their nations, they were received with great ceremony at court. Queens played an important role in the formal reception of ambassadors—this was a key opportunity for image crafting and display as ambassadors sent word home of the manner in which they were received, the behaviour of the queen, and the glamour and wealth of the court. Mary Queen of Scots combined the ceremonial element of receiving ambassadors with magnificent court celebrations designed to impress her visitors such as masquing, banquets, and hunts.

Other court rituals were connected to distinctive cultural practices and values. One of the main ceremonies for Korean queens was the annual sericulture ceremony each spring, where the queen enacted a symbolic representation of all women's work. This ritual involved the queen and her entourage of elite women making an offering to the goddess of silkworms, ritually plucking a mulberry tree, and then depositing the leaves at the silkworm rearing room before changing into ceremonial robes for a formal banquet for the participants. Finally, the king would host another feast for the queen, attended by his officials who thanked her for her labour and congratulated her for the successful performance

---

15 Zach Zorich, "Uncovering a Maya Warrior Queen," *Archaeology* 66, no. 3 (2013): 31–35 at 35.

16 Nakanyike B. Musisi, "Women, 'Elite Polygyny' and Buganda State Formation," *Signs* 16, no. 4 (1991): 757–86 at 781–82.

of the ritual (Shin, 109–13). Rainmaking rituals or ceremonial to ensure a good harvest were also key rituals in many countries, as part of the role of the monarchy to act as a mediator between their subjects and the divine. In Africa, several examples exist of monarchies which have strong traditions regarding the powers of kings and queens who have the power to bring rain through their personal magic and the performance of ritual both historically and in the present day. Perhaps the most famous of these, in terms of women, is the Rain Queen of the Lovedu who performs an annual rainmaking ritual—these regnant queens have followed a strict line of matrilineal succession from the beginning of the nineteenth century up to the present day to retain the rainmaking powers in their family. However, in other monarchies in Africa queens consort and queen mothers can also perform rainmaking rituals. Indeed, part of the selection criteria for brides of Lotuho kings (in South Sudan) is that both of her parents "have rain"—if her parents were not of rain descent, she cannot be a full or "red" queen (Simonse, 226 and 301–2). This rainmaking ability is viewed as crucial for it falls to her to be not only the guardian of the heir if the king dies, but the custodian of the rainmaking magic and ritual stones.

Major lifecycle events in a queen's life are often tied to important ceremonial events—as noted previously, these trace the trajectory of their lives from baptism, betrothals and weddings, coronation, childbirth related ceremonial, and finally to their funeral. The first ceremonial which a royal woman participated in was often linked to her own birth— while she was the focus of these events, she could not be a fully engaged participant. This ceremonial could be quite elaborate, as the birth of any royal child was an occasion which reinforced dynastic continuity. For example, the christening of Princess Beatrice, the fifth daughter of Victoria of the United Kingdom, on June 16, 1857 in the royal chapel at Buckingham Palace, was an impressive occasion. The Archbishop of Canterbury conducted the ceremony, there was a musical performance with an anthem which had been written expressly for the occasion and meal in the palace ballroom for the royal family and their exalted guests. However, in some cultures and courts, the birth of a princess—or indeed any child who was not designated as the heir—did not trigger such elaborate ceremony, only basic rituals for any infant's safe delivery.

Due to the significance of a royal woman's marriage in building dynastic alliances and in establishing her own position, there was considerable ceremonial from the initial betrothal or selection of the bride through to the wedding itself. In addition, celebrations connected to matrimonial ceremonies could last for days, or even weeks, around the date of the actual wedding itself including feasts, jousting, firework displays, plays, pageants, and more. Far from just celebrating the union of a royal couple, the ceremonial and celebratory events around a wedding could serve multiple political purposes—Philip II of Macedon made the wedding of his daughter Cleopatra into a Panhellenic festival, to showcase his wealth and power and "emphasized the nearly divine specialness of the royal house" (Carney, 205).

As noted earlier, a princess might be betrothed several times over her youth and thus take part in a number of ceremonies, or she may be very young when first promised to wed. Mary Tudor, daughter of Henry VIII, was only two years old when she was betrothed with lavish ceremony to the French dauphin in October 1518—the prospective groom was even younger, only seven months old, and so was represented by the French ambassador as he was too young to take part. In premodern Europe, queens often had multiple weddings—first a proxy wedding, in which representatives for the bride and/or groom took part in a ritual which was more binding than just the betrothal, to give more security to both parties that the union would go ahead. Yet, as consummation was vital to validate the marriage, some proxy ceremonies had a mock bedding element where the stand ins for the bride and/or groom would either lie next to each other in bed and touch their legs briefly together or even just sit next to each other in bed to satisfy the notion that the marriage was consummated.

Another key stage in the ceremonial around royal weddings involved the bride's journey to her new home and celebrations for her arrival. This began to be an important feature during the Hellenistic Era, as it increased the prominence and political benefits of the event by allowing it to reach a much larger audience. Renaissance Europe, where royal entries and progresses were important urban rituals, offers many examples of bridal entries which were often memorialized in festival books or other printed accounts for wider consumption, like the sixteenth-century *Receipt of the Lady Katherine* which recounts the arrival of Catherine of Aragon in England. Bridal entries also gave the public an opportunity to express ideals of queenship—Anna of Denmark's entry to Edinburgh had a number of pageants including one with "five speakers representing Virtue and her daughters, Prudence, Justice, Fortitude and Temperance [...] Virtue proclaimed that any queen who incorporates these four daughters into the development of her own character would rule well, while those who ignore her offspring's virtues would ultimately descend into ruin."[17] A bridal journey could be lengthy with many stops en route, such as Anne de Foix–Candale's trip from France to Hungary via northern Italy in 1502, Margaret Tudor's journey across the length of England to Scotland in 1503, or Elisabeth de Valois' series of ceremonial entries to Spanish cities including Pamplona, Guadalajara, Alcala, and Madrid in 1559. Bridal journeys could have other significant cultural meanings—for example, in Lotuho royal brides had to "follow the itinerary by which the culture hero and royal ancestor, Imuhunyi, entered Lotuholand. She pays a visit to all of the villages until the site of ancient Imatari is reached [...] the sacred hill for the Lotuho kingdom" (account from Novelli, cited in Simonse, 226).

---

17 Lucinda H. S. Dean, "Enter the Alien: Foreign Consorts and their Royal Entries into Scottish Cities c. 1449–1560," in *Ceremonial Entries in Early Modern Europe: The Iconography of Power*, ed. J. R. Mulryne, Maria Ines Aliverti, and Anna Maria Testaverde (Aldershot: Ashgate, 2015), 267–95 at 273.

For Christian queens, their actual wedding ceremony invariably included a religious element, whether the ceremonial was performed in front of or within a church or in a royal chapel, a form of blessing took place from a prelate to recognize and validate the couple's union. As noted previously however, consummation was a vital element to make the marriage fully legitimate and legally binding. Indeed, non-consummation was often cited in the annulment of a royal marriage, although this could be hotly disputed as in the case of Louis XII and Jeanne de France in 1498 or that of Henry VIII and Catherine of Aragon, as a key element in the validity of their marriage was whether or not she and Henry's brother Arthur, Prince of Wales, had sex. Due to the heightened significance of consummation in Poland it "was explicitly performed as an affair of state" with elaborate ceremonial of its own to provide witnesses that the couple had been put to bed together.[18] Ultimately, whether consummation was directly witnessed, indirectly observed by listening outside the bedchamber, or some kind of proof such as stained sheets was given, it was important to complete the wedding ceremonial with this final ritual element to ensure that the union would be binding—and hopefully lead to the desired result of heirs to provide dynastic continuity.

In Africa, however, other rituals were used to affirm the validity of a royal union. In South Sudan, the Lulubo king and his bride were placed together in a small hut where an ebony fire was burning—as the smoke of ebony wood is particularly acrid, it was a key test to see if one of them reacted badly to the fumes by sneezing. If they did so, it was believed to be an indication that they were unfit for the royal position, or that "the office does not like them" (Simonse, 225–26). If they did withstand the smoke, then the ceremonial to affirm their union was completed with a sacrifice of purification—the queen would then assume her office and her bridewealth would be paid. Swazi kings did not normally pay bridewealth,

---

18 Katarzyna Kosior, *Becoming a Queen in Early Modern Europe* (New York: Palgrave Macmillan, 2019), 143.

with the exception of the wife or first queen who was designated to bear the royal heir and thus would eventually
become the queen mother, or most powerful woman in the
realm. Because of her importance, her bridewealth was paid
from the royal herd or *mfukwane*, which symbolized the whole
nation and was so sacred that it was believed that only the
king, queen mother, and first queen could come into contact
with the fat of these animals and stay sane.[19] Normally, Swazi
brides were smeared with red clay during the course of wedding rituals, but the first queen was smeared with the dung
of the royal herd instead to recognize her bond with them
and the realm as the mother of the nation. The significance
of cattle can also be seen in a "bedding" ritual of the Lotuho,
where the king and queen spent their first night together on
the skin of a special black bull who has come from the village
of Lobera and whose flesh has been ritually consumed by the
monyomiji or elites—this ritual not only confirms their union
but ensures the prosperity of the whole realm (Simonse, 226).

Joseon Korea offers an example of elaborate ceremonial for royal weddings, which had to be followed in a strict
sequence and according to detailed protocol, for the union
to be considered to be valid. The bride was selected after
an extensive screening process—once that decision was
made, there was a ten-step process of rituals which had
to be completed before she was properly wed. First rituals
were conducted to select an auspicious date and then the
bride's family was ceremonially informed. Rather than a ritual
which focused on uniting the royal couple, the key moment
was effectively the bride's investiture in her new office. This
important *chaekbi* ceremony was held at a special bridal
pavilion where she was given her official document of investiture, her seal of office, and "mandate robes" or *myeongbok*;
at this point she was regarded as the queen (Shin, 89). The
induction ritual or *myeongsa-bongyeong* followed where the
queen was escorted into the palace by a sizeable procession

---

19 T. O. Beidelman, "Swazi Royal Ritual," *Africa: Journal of the
International African Institute* 36, no. 4 (1966): 373–405 at 383 and 393.

of courtiers, officials, and royal family members. Finally, the *dongroe* or consummation ritual took place on the queen's first night at the palace, if she and the groom were of suitable age. While this completed the major ceremonies, more rituals followed for the new bride to present her formally to the royal family, the court, the officials, and the wives of the major clans of the realm.

Byzantine empresses similarly had to be invested in office before they wed—it was necessary for her to be elevated and sanctified through the religious ceremony where she was ritually garbed in the imperial cloak of office to "achieve sacredness before she became [the emperor's] wife."[20] Yet for many royal women their wedding came before any ceremony of installation or coronation. Not all consorts had a formal ceremony to recognize their ascension to the queen's office—for consorts it was not always necessary that they undergo a coronation, investiture, or installation but their position was certainly enhanced by the formal recognition of their status through these important rituals. However, regnant queens were required to undergo a ceremony to mark the beginning of their reign, which varied according to the monarchical traditions of the realm. Often these traditions, which had been designed with a male sovereign in mind would have to be modified to accommodate a female ruler—this could be even more complicated if the queen was married, as the coronation ceremonies would have to be adjusted to include a king consort as well. An example of this can be seen in the coronation for Juana II of Navarre in 1329—the traditional Navarrese ritual called for the sovereign to be raised up on a shield while the onlookers cried "Real! Real! Real!"[21] When plans were being drawn up for Juana's coronation—the first performed for a regnant queen in the realm—they intended for the queen to be raised up alone as the rightful heiress. However, her husband Philip d'Evreux strenuously objected

20 Åsa Boholm, "The Coronation of Female Death: The Dogaressa of Venice," *Man* 27, no. 1 (1992): 91–104 at 95.

21 Woodacre, *Queens Regnant*, 61–63.

to this plan which he felt would preclude his involvement in the governance of the realm—ultimately, both the queen and her husband were raised on the shield together to reflect their ruling partnership.

Queens consort could also share a coronation with their husbands—if she was already married to the heir, she might share in the ceremonial for her husband's elevation to the throne. The queen could play a prominent role in their joint installation; for example a Khmer chronicle recounts a joint coronation from the seventeenth century where the queen was responsible for placing not just the scroll with her own title, but also the one bearing her husband's, onto a ceremonial tray, confirming their position as the new rulers.[22] African monarchies show many different scenarios for coronation rit uals, many of which featured both king and his consort or his chief wife. For example, in Buganda, the king and his queen sister, or *lubuga*, are installed jointly, being carried together to a sacred site at Budo Hill where they participate equally in the ceremony, taking oaths to defend the realm. However, as noted previously, in many polygamous courts, queen mothers could be the most powerful and exalted woman in the realm and thus she could be the one to share a coronation ceremony with the new king, as in the case of the Swazi when the king and the queen mother are installed in office together.

Queenly coronations could also be individual events—for example, almost all of the queens consort in fourteenth and fifteenth-century England, from Philippa of Hainault in 1330 to Elizabeth of York in 1486, received a solo coronation, with the exception of Anne Neville, who was crowned alongside her husband Richard III in 1483. Indeed, Philippa of Hainault and Elizabeth of York exemplify the situation of some consorts who only received coronations once they had produced, or were pregnant with, an heir. Ceremonies for a consort's installation could also be restricted by gender, taking place in a purely female environment, as in the case of the inves-

---

22 Barbara Watson Andaya, "Women and Power in Southeast Asia," in *Servants of the Dynasty*, ed. Walthall, 37.

titure of Chinese empresses where only titled ladies and female officials took part in the ritual—even the celebratory banquets were segregated, with one for the emperor and his officials and another for the empresses and her ladies.[23]

Childbirth was another major focus for ritual and ceremony in the lifecycle of a queen. Effectively the process of queenly childbirth and the attendant ceremonial can be broken down into three key stages: pregnancy, childbirth, and post-partum. Given the vital role that the queen played as the mother of heirs and guarantor of dynastic continuity, her pregnancies were closely observed to ensure that all went well. For example, in Lotuho, once the queen was pregnant a state of *edwar*, or non-violence, was declared which even banned dancing and drumming, to ensure the development and safe delivery of the child she carried (Simonse, 226). Joseon queens also worked to ensure the positive development of their child in womb by ensuring that their thoughts were pure and that they were not exposed to improper behaviour or unclean food (Shin, 92). Given the somewhat tenuous nature of the early stages of pregnancy, the early rituals to ensure a healthy pregnancy could be more private—in the case of the late twelfth-century Japanese consort Taira no Tokushi, it was the empress and her family who sponsored rituals and offerings outside the setting of the imperial court. Due to those same concerns about the uncertainty of pregnancy, in European courts there was not always a ceremonial event to announce the queen's pregnancy—the royal family might prefer to communicate the news across their dynastic networks and wait until their body's changing shape made the pregnancy apparent at court (Kosior, 148–49). In contrast, at the Japanese court, the announcement of the empress's pregnancy was heralded by a significant ceremony to don the sash of maternity. This ceremony took place in the fifth month of pregnancy—the sash, which was believed to secure the baby's position in the womb and ensure a safe delivery, was prepared by the empress's family and tied around her waist by the emperor as a means of claiming the child's paternity.[24] This sash donning ceremony initiated a series of rituals to follow, from daily purification rituals in the imperial palace to Buddhist esoteric rituals and sutra recitations sponsored by the empress and her family at various temples and shrines. At the Joseon court, once the queen's pregnancy was confirmed a special "Delivery Office" was set up with doctors, midwives, and officials whose role was to monitor baby and mother and to prepare for the birth itself as well as conduct all related ceremonial.

Across various cultures, queens normally gave birth in a designated space which was ritually prepared for the important event. This could be tied to a particular location due to meaning, for example Henry VII was keen for Elizabeth of York to give birth to their son at Winchester in 1486 because of its long history of important royal ceremonies. Combining this significant birthplace with the name Arthur for the infant heir which harked back to a legendary king, aided the symbolic establishment of the new Tudor dynasty through these ancient royal connections. Location could have significance for other reasons—in imperial Japan, it was critical that the consort give birth outside the palace to protect the emperor from being harmed by the pollution of the childbirth process, thus the consort would withdraw to a mansion within the capital a few months before her due date. However, Korean queens and their European counterparts generally gave birth at a royal residence in a room or area of their apartments which had been prepared for their confinement and delivery. A common practice amongst many courts was to ensure that the birthing room was well appointed with ritual objects which were believed to offer spiritual protection for mother and child. Christ's foreskin was brought to Isabeau of Bavaria, queen of France, for each of her deliveries, while talismans

---

24 Naoko Gunji, "Taira no Tokushi's Birth of the Emperor Antoku," in *Women, Rites and Ritual Objects in Premodern Japan*, ed. Karen M. Gerhart (Leiden: Brill, 2018), 89–137 at 96–98.

and charms featured in Joseon Korea and Buddhist icons and statues were made for Taira no Tokushi.[25]

Given the significance of the potential outcome of the birth—the production of a future monarch—once a queen went into labour, many attendants and observers could be called, including religious personnel who performed important rituals and courtiers and officials to witness and verify the birth. However, while dozens of servants, politicians, courtiers, and royal family members witnessed Mary of Modena give birth to a son in 1688, the contradictory accounts of observers could not conclusively refute rumours that the child had been smuggled in a warming pan.[26] During the labour of a Japanese imperial consort, a flurry of different religious practitioners arrived to perform rituals to ensure a positive outcome—one twelfth-century account described the chanting of sutras by Buddhist monks, Shinto priests, and yin-yang diviners performing offerings, ascetics-exorcists conducting *kaji* prayers to purify the house, and esoteric masters performing a ritual to remove evil spirits and assist childbirth by rubbing her abdomen with purified ox bezoar.[27]

Immediately after the birth it was vital to ensure that the baby thrived and that the mother regained her health after the ordeal. Thus, royal mothers remained in confinement during this period and extensive rituals focused on purification and protection were conducted to ensure the wellbeing of mother and baby and mitigate the pollution believed

---

25 Murielle Gaude-Ferragu, *Queenship in Medieval France, 1300-1500* (New York: Palgrave McMillan, 2016), 57.

26 Lisa Forman Cody, *Birthing the Nation: Sex, Science and the Conception of Eighteenth Century Britons* (Oxford: Oxford University Press, 2005), 71–78.

27 Selections from "Procedures During the Day of the Royal Consort's Labour," in Anna Andreeva, "Childbirth in Early Medieval Japan: Ritual Economies and Medical Emergencies in Procedures During the Day of the Royal Consort's Labour," in *Buddhism and Medicine: An Anthology of Premodern Sources*, ed. C. Pierce Salguero (New York: Columbia University Press, 2017), 340–41.

to permeate the process of childbirth. In Japan and Korea, the confinement lasted for seven days—both cultures had a special bathing ceremony for mother and baby, in Japan this occurred daily for seven days while in Korea this was done on the third day after the birth. On the seventh day after the birth in Korea a special "Remove the Straw" ceremony was performed which involved the ritual removal and storage of the birthing bed and a sacrifice with offerings of silk, silver, and rice, along with special rituals to clean and store the umbilical cord and placenta in a special urn. At this point if mother and baby were well and the rituals had all been performed, the "Delivery Office" for the royal birth was closed (Shin, 94–95).

For many European consorts, their period of confinement was concluded with a religious ceremony which ritually purified them and welcomed them back into the wider world. The feast of Candlemas held forty days after the birth of Christ is also a celebration of the Purification of the Virgin, thus the lying-in period for many Christian queens followed this same forty-day pattern (Gaude-Ferragu, 61). However, there was some variance in this—the Old Testament stipulated thirty-three days after the birth of a boy and sixty-six after the birth of a girl, but Pope Gregory declared there was no fixed date when a woman could return to church after delivery.[28] Whether confinement lasted a month after the birth or slightly longer, it was ample time to ensure that both mother and child had survived and thus the ceremony served as both a means of purification and thanksgiving for her safe delivery. In medieval France, the ceremony was held in the royal chapel and included a full mass after which the queen would be sprinkled with holy water by the priest as a means of purification and then she made a ritual offering of a candle with a coin embedded in it, bread, and wine—a feast followed

---

28 Sue Nierbrzydowski, "*Asperges me, Domine, hyssopo*: Male Voice, Female Interpretation and the Medieval English Purification of Women after Childbirth Ceremony," *Early Music* 39, no. 3 (2011): 327–34 at 327–28.

the ceremony to celebrate the queen's return to the court (Gaude-Ferragu, 62–63).

However, many queens did not survive the process of childbirth or died shortly thereafter from complications or infections, such as the English queen Jane Seymour or the Mughal empress Mumtaz Muhal, whose death prompted the construction of the famous Taj Mahal. The death of queens triggered the last ceremony performed in their honour, their funeral, which offers us an opportunity to draw together the three elements discussed in this chapter—patronage, display, and ritual—and examine how death was a final opportunity for a queen to craft her image. A queen could cement her role as patroness of a religious institution by building her tomb there and her final will and testament (if she was able to make one), was an opportunity to direct her funds to support institutions she valued as well as demonstrate her wide-ranging network of connections by making bequests from her collection of books, jewellery, relics, and other material goods—which would all enhance her legacy. Yet the ability of queens to manage their image after death was limited— plans put into place during her lifetime or in her will could be scuppered by surviving family members, or successors, who sought to erase her accomplishments or craft an image of her life which was more beneficial to their own purposes. An idealized image of the queen could be created by herself or by others—while this image might mirror ideals of queenly comportment, it may not be a true reflection of the woman, her life, and her exercise of the office. The rituals and com- memoration of the late queen were also an opportunity for the dynasty to glorify itself by highlighting her importance as progenitor to stress dynastic continuity and their links to other dynasties through her to demonstrate their wider polit- ical significance.

The ceremonial connected to the death and burial of queens has had great significance as long as monarchy itself has existed. Records survive of the rituals performed for ancient Assyrian queens which note the role of the queen's daughter and the other women of the royal harem who cried

"Come bury the queen, the daughter of righteousness!"[29]
While funeral ceremonies vary over time, place, culture, and
religion, we can see three key elements which link across the
deaths of most queens: cleansing of the body after death
(which may include a period of resting or "lying in state"),
a religious ceremony, and internment or cremation. Another
element shared in many queenly funerals is a procession to
their final resting place, which may take place before or after
the religious ceremony. In 1514, Anne de Bretagne had a ten
day procession of her coffin from Blois to Paris with nightly
stops along the way in several towns where vigils for the dead
were prayed for her, bells were rung, and requiems read for
her soul.[30] The magnificence of a funeral procession can
reflect a queen's power and influence—the Ottoman *valide
sultan* Nurbanu, who had been regent for her son Murad III
was accorded ceremonial befitting of a ruler when she died in
1583—her procession included "the magnificent ulema, hon-
ourable sheiks, and functionaries of state, all on foot along
the sides of the coffin, and the Padishah, Protector of the
World, clad in a robe of mourning and in tears [...]."[31] Expres-
sions of royal and courtly grief were also a common element
in the records of queenly deaths, such as the twelfth-century Caliph al-Nasir of Baghdad who was "so grief stricken
at her [Sajuqi Khatun] passing that he could not eat or drink
for days" and left her residence sealed up as it was when she
died for several years.[32]

---

29 "The Burial of a Queen," in *State Archives of Assyria. Volume XX:
Assyrian Royal Rituals and Cultic Texts*, ed. Simo Parpola (Helsinki:
The Neo-Assyrian Text Corpus Project, 2017), 93–95.

30 See Hélène M. Bloem, "The Processions and Decorations at the
Royal Funeral of Anne of Brittany," *Bibliothèque d'Humanisme et
Renaissance* 54, no. 1 (1992): 131–60.

31 "Selânikî," in Pinar Kayaalp, *The Empress Nurbanu and Ottoman
Politics in the Sixteenth Century* (London: Routledge, 2018), 37.

32 Ibn al-Sa'I, *Consorts of the Caliphs: Women and the Court of
Baghdad*, trans. Shawkat M. Toorawa (New York: NYU Press, 2017), 69.

The expense of an elaborate funeral ceremony for a queen, in combination with the significant financial outlay for her tomb and the goods buried with her, all underscored the importance of both the woman herself and the office that she held. Often, it is the combination of the magnitude and magnificence of the items buried with her that identify a tomb as that of a queen—the tomb of one Silla (Korean) royal woman from the fourth century CE, believed to be that of Queen Poban, contained golden artefacts weighing more than four kilos in total, including a gold crown covered in jade.[33] Similarly, the primary chamber of Tomb 800 at the Royal Cemetery at Ur, believed to be that of Queen Puabi from the mid-third millennium BCE, contained the queen's body which was covered in jewellery and adornments made from gold, silver, and precious stones, including an elaborate headdress—as well as the bodies of sacrificed attendants, presumably to serve the queen in the afterlife.[34] These grave goods, including the remains of the queen's household, serve as perhaps the ultimate manifestation of display—demonstrating the queen's exalted status, wealth, and power in life, death, and the afterlife to ensure that they have a long lasting legacy.

A queen's tomb is the final expression of patronage, display, and ritual—it often becomes the most enduring expression of her image. The commissioning of tombs can be seen as an important form of artistic, religious, and monumental patronage for queens. Indeed, queens played a significant role as the guardians of family memory and dynastic imagery through their engagement in the creation and management of a royal necropolis. Queens commissioned tombs for themselves and for others—for example, Joan of Navarre commissioned a tomb for her first husband, Jean IV of Brittany, after

---

33 Sarah Milledge Nelson, "The Queens of Silla: Power and Connections to the Spirit World," in *Ancient Queens*, ed. Nelson, 85–87.

34 Amy R. Gansell, "Women in Ancient Mesopotamia," in *A Companion to Women in the Ancient World*, ed. James and Dillon, 13–16.

his death in 1399 and later commissioned a joint tomb for herself and her second husband, Henry IV of England, at Canterbury Cathedral. The Egyptian pharaoh Hatshepsut commissioned two tombs for herself and a massive mortuary temple at Deir el-Bahri—the first tomb was designed for her role as consort but later, when she assumed regent and then regnant role, her more elevated status required a tomb and temple fitting for a pharaoh. Her temple was designed to perpetuate her mortuary cult to secure her afterlife as well as secure her legacy through the building's iconography which was designed to make a strong statement during her lifetime and beyond that she was a legitimate pharaoh, not a mere regent for or usurper of Thutmose III. Yet after her death, Thutmose destroyed representations of Hatshepsut, chiselling off insignias of power from her statues and removing her cartouches in an effort to undo the queen's efforts to create an image herself as a powerful pharaoh. This demonstrates the lack of control that many queens had over their funerary monuments after their death and the ways in which their successors could alter the image that they had so carefully crafted in life. For example, James VI and I decided to move the tomb of his mother, Mary Queen of Scots, from Peterborough Cathedral to Westminster Abbey, even though her own wishes were to be buried in France. James placed his mother directly across the Lady Chapel from the tomb he built for his cousin and predecessor, Elizabeth I—who was responsible for Mary's execution for her many plots to assume Elizabeth's throne. Elizabeth, in turn, was buried directly on top of her sister and predecessor, Mary I, whose tomb has little beyond the inscription to identify it as hers as the tomb bears only Elizabeth's effigy. While this tomb building program served James's purposes by installing his mother among her Tudor family, thus underlining his own legitimacy and rehabilitating her memory, the placement of their tombs was not necessarily what any of the three regnant queens would have designed for themselves.

Three key elements of a tomb are critical for image projection: the location, the type of tomb, and the decoration. Many queens chose to be buried at sites connected to their patronage, reinforcing their memory as patroness—such as Isabel of Aragon, queen of Portugal, who was buried at the monastery of Santa Clara-a-Velha that she founded or Mahperi Khatun whose tomb is located in the mosque complex she built in the Anatolian city of Kayseri in the thirteenth century. Another option was to be buried in a royal necropolis—this could reflect a queen's desire, or that of their surviving husband and/or children, to underline their dynastic connections and her role as daughter and sister and/or wife, mother, and matriarch. A queen consort was more likely to feature in a royal necropolis if she was buried in a joint tomb with her husband as his position would often drive decisions about location and the iconography of their tomb. However, there was an additional option—a "divided" burial, where parts of the body were buried elsewhere, giving a queen the opportunity to link herself in death with multiple meaningful locations. While this became less popular with Christian queens after the practice was banned by Pope Boniface VIII in 1299, Anne de Bretagne still chose to have her heart removed and buried in Brittany, where she had been sovereign duchess, even though her body was buried with her second husband Louis XII of France at the royal necropolis of St. Denis. However, it is important to note that some queens were moved after death—their remains may have been translated or reburied by their descendants, or impacted by natural disasters such as floods and earthquakes or even by wars and revolutions which could destroy their funerary monuments, or remove them from their intended locational context—for example when they have been placed in modern museums today.

Finally, the visual elements of the tomb, including the effigy, decoration, and inscription, were a vital canvas for projecting the queen's image and cementing it in memory. The queen's effigy—both on the tomb and the one which may have been used in her funeral procession—links back to the earlier discussion of portraiture as a means of image crafting. However, while effigies used in funeral processions could often be quite lifelike, those which featured on the queen's tomb or sarcophagus were often idealized, again reflecting an ideal of beauty or a traditional template, rather than the features of the woman herself. In some cultures, there is no element of portraiture in a funeral monument—Islamic tombs can be simple and unadorned or have beautiful decorative elements and calligraphy but there can be no depiction of the individual's image. In addition, some cultures use stele, gravemarkers, or other monuments instead of tombs—these can feature a depiction of the woman herself, like the stela of the eighth-century Mayan queen Ix Mutal Ahaw wearing a magnificent headdress or may feature little or no decoration at all, like the famously "blank" funerary stela of Wu Zetian.

The tomb or monument's decoration can also send a strong message about the queen's life, family, and accomplishments. Heraldry was a powerful means of demonstrating a queen's dynastic identity, such as the lions rampant on the tomb of Leonor Plantagenet at Las Huelgas de Burgos which underscored her role as an English princess as well as a Castilian queen by marriage. The iconography and inscription could serve an important role in a queen's legacy after death by demonstrating how her life had been spent in a perfect reflection of queenly ideals and virtues. For example, the tomb of Maria of Hungary, a fourteenth-century queen of Naples, demonstrates her piety as the queen is depicted with the Virgin Mary, Queen of Heaven—who intercedes on Maria's behalf to recommend her to Christ. Maria's religious patronage is stressed by an angel who holds a model of the church she founded, Santa Maria Donna Regina, in his arms. Her fertility and role as dynastic progenitor are demonstrated by the depiction of her sons, including the king Charles Martel and St. Louis of Toulouse. Finally, her sarcophagus is supported by depictions of the four cardinal virtues: Prudence, Temperance, Justice, and Fortitude—emphasizing her virtuous behaviour in life.[35] Inscriptions can also be a useful means of

---

35 Tanja Michalsky, "Mater serenissimi principis: The Tomb of Maria of Hungary," in *The Church of Santa Maria Donna Regina: Art, Iconography, and Patronage in Fourteenth-Century Naples*, ed. Janis Elliott and Cordelia Warr (Aldershot: Ashgate, 2004), 61–77.

highlighting a queen's role as a virtuous exemplar—the cenotaph of Mahperi Khatun notes:

> This is the tomb of the lady, the veiled, the fortunate, the happy, "the martyr" (*al-shahida*), the ascetic, the obedient, the fighter, the promoter of faith, the chaste, the just, "queen of the women in the world" (*al-malika al-nisa' fi'l-'alam*), the virtuous and clean, "the Mary of her age" (*Maryam awaniha*), "the Khadija of her time" (*Khadija zamaniha*), "possessor of knowledge, almsgiver of wealth in thousands" (*sahibat al-mar'ufa al-mutasaddiqa bi'l-mal uluf*), "purity of the world and religion."[36]

This brings us neatly full circle through this expression of the myriad of virtues and qualities that queens were expected to possess, as discussed at the outset of this volume. As we have seen in this chapter patronage, display, and ceremonial were crucial elements in image construction. A queen's actions—such as founding and supporting religious institutions, displaying their status through their majestic apparel, and performance of ritual and ceremonial on both a daily and extraordinary basis—both reflected and reinforced expectations of queenly behaviour. Their memorials lauded their achievements as a ruler or consort, their familial roles, exalted rank, and dynastic connections and their impeccable virtues—in some ways, telling us less about the individual woman and more about being a queen.

---

36 Suzan Yalman, "The 'Dual Identity' of Mahperi Khatun: Piety, Patronage and Marriage across Frontiers in Seljuk Anatolia," in *Architecture and Landscape in Medieval Anatolia, 1100–1500*, ed. Patricia Blessing and Rachel Goshgarian (Edinburgh: Edinburgh University Press, 2017), 224–52 at 230–31.

Conclusion

At the end of the last chapter, we returned to where we began by reflecting on the ideals of queens and the expectations of the practice of queenship. By taking a global perspective, we have been able to see the similarities over time, culture, and place in the extensive list of virtues that queens were meant to possess and model to their subjects including being pious, humble, wise, peacemaking, and chaste. A continuous feedback loop reinforces these ideals—first from society communicating these expectations to queens through textual sources such as conduct literature and "Mirrors for Queens" to performative aspects such as pageants in royal or bridal entries through to praise of "perfect" queens or criticism of women who contravene these expectations. This input feeds into the both the education of royal women and shapes their actions to model these virtues and create an image that aims to resonate with these expectations. This leaves a positive legacy or a negative "black legend" which in turn reinforces these ideals to society, creating more material to be incorporated into biographies of queenly "worthies" or "anti-worthies" which then inform the upbringing of future queens.

The wide-ranging perspective of this work has also demonstrated the similarities in terms of how family creates the basis of a royal woman's authority through the key roles that queens play throughout their lifecycle, as vital pawns in dynastic matrimonial diplomacy, as co-rulers with their husbands and other family members and as powerful mothers and matriarchs. It has demonstrated their agency and activity in rule through effective networking and administration, war and peace, financial management, and cultural influence. We have noted the struggles that women faced, and overcame, as heiresses and unorthodox successors to become rulers in their own right as well as the various forms of co-rulership and regency that granted queens significant power and authority on every continent and in every era of history. Finally, we have seen how patronage, ceremonial, and display underpin the queen's role both as key aspects of the exercise of queenship and as a means to craft an image which could support her reign and dynasty as well as leave a lasting legacy.

Yet, while considerable continuity in the theory and practice of queenship has been demonstrated across time and place, this global survey has also revealed some interesting differences in the experiences of royal women. The pivotal dividing line can be seen in matrimonial practices, between monogamous and polygamous court environments. Interestingly, though the bulk of queenship research has been focused on premodern, Christian Europe where monogamy has prevailed for millennia, the majority of royal women have experienced queenship in a polygamous context. This key difference has a knock-on effect in several areas as discussed throughout this work. In the first instance, if a monarch has many wives or sexual partners, it introduces an element of competition among these women for pre-eminence by becoming the favourite, the mother of the heir, or the one who holds the premier title. While one woman might be able to successfully attain all of these distinctions at once, it was also possible to have, for example, an empress, another consort who was the biological mother of the heir, and a concubine who dominated the emperor's attention and affection, along with a host of other women who all sought to attain their places. While a European queen may have to compete with a royal mistress for her husband's affections or may not be the mother of the heir if she was childless or the second wife, she never had to worry about a large harem of other potential partners who could unseat her by usurping her place in her husband's affections and even her position at any given time. Another key differential that has been noted in a polygamous scenario is that more emphasis, and power, is given to the sovereign's mother—while the monarch could have many wives and many women might bear him heirs, he could only have one mother. Thus, while many European royal mothers were able to wield power as regents or by influencing their ruling children, the polygamous framework clearly put more weight on matriarchs as the first woman at court rather than the consort—from Ottoman *valide sultans* to Chinese dowager empresses to Swazi queen mothers who were literally enthroned with their sons as their ruling partners. A final difference is the issue of access and visibility—however, it would be a mistake to assume that all polygamous courts practised *purdah* or cloistered their women. The issue of queenly visibility and the accessibility of her quarters, or that of the women of the palace, varied considerably between different cultural settings. Moreover, as has been demonstrated earlier, physical barriers which reduced a royal woman's visibility did not create a barrier to her political influence or authority, from Korean regents who ruled from "behind the bamboo curtain" to the Hapsburg empress Maria of Austria who wielded considerable influence while ostensibly cloistered in the convent of Descalzas Reales in Madrid.

It is precisely by shifting the focus, from the specific and local to the timeless and global, that we can begin to see the bigger picture of queenship and draw important connections across time and place which improve our understanding of the life and office of the queen. While the growth of queenship studies as a field has shed considerable light on lives of premodern European queens, the wider context of royal women's experience in different periods, places, and cultures has only just begun to be comparatively explored. By bringing together the existing studies of particular queens and queenship in various settings and combining the work of historians, anthropologists, literary scholars, archaeologists, art historians, and other specialists, we can develop a much richer understanding of the vital place of women in monarchy which helps us in turn to ask different questions to drive research in the field of queenship studies ever onwards.

Finally, this work began by asking why we should study queens and what relevance queenship studies had in this modern era. While this book has focused on royal women largely from the premodern era, it has demonstrated the intensive political and cultural agency of queens across time and place, highlighting their central role in their societies and their influence on the history and development of their realms. This has continuing relevance today on multiple fronts. First, monarchy as an institution is still in operation today—while this has evolved to become more symbolic than autocratic in nature, queens regnant, consort, and dowager are highly visible in today's society. Moreover, their role, and by extension the ideals and practice of queenship, is a topic of discussion and debate today, from the conflict over female successors in Java, Japan, and for the Lovedu rain queen, and indeed in the promulgation of the Succession to the Crown Act in Britain in 2013 which finally eliminated male primogeniture in the United Kingdom. The partnership of regnant queens and consort kings has also been closely observed from the seventy-three-year long marriage of Elizabeth II of the United Kingdom and the duke of Edinburgh to the wedding of the Crown Princess Victoria of Sweden to her former personal trainer, Daniel Westling, in 2010. There has been intensive scrutiny of women with a non-aristocratic background like Queen Letizia of Spain, a former newsreader, and Catherine, duchess of Cambridge, or even her sister-in-law, Meghan Markle, duchess of Sussex, regarding how they adapt to or eschew their royal role and connect with their subjects' expectations of their behaviour, dress, and execution of their duties. Powerful regents and queen mothers can still be seen today, particularly in African monarchies as Queen Ntfombi of Swaziland illustrates as first regent for and now co-ruler with her son Mswati III. Thus, the key concepts of this examination of queens and queenship in historical context provides a key framework for understanding the experience and expectations of royal women today. Secondly, beyond the setting of monarchy, the activities and agency of the queens discussed in this work demonstrate that the current wave of female politicians and world leaders, ostensibly driven by the rise of feminism, owes a great debt to a foundation built by several millennia of politically savvy and powerful royal women.

Further Reading

Amirell, Stefan. "Female Rule in the Indian Ocean World (1300–1900)," *Journal of World History* 26, no. 3 (2015), 443–89.
> An excellent overview of female rulership in this geographical context with a helpful appendix which lists all of the female sovereigns across the region.

Andaya, Barbara Watson. *The Flaming Womb: Repositioning Women in Early Modern Southeast Asia.* Honolulu: University of Hawaii Press, 2006.
> See chapter 6, "Women, Courts and Class," for an excellent overview of royal women across this region during the early modern period.

Beem, Charles. *Queenship in Early Modern Europe.* London: Red Globe, 2020.
> A very engaging textbook on early modern queenship—useful for students and approachable for those new to the subject.

Buijs, Gina. "Ritual Sisters or Female Rulers? Gender and Chiefship Revisited in Southern Africa." In *Identity and Networks: Fashioning Gender and Ethnicity Across Cultures*, edited by Deborah Fahy Bryceson, Judith Okely, and Jonathan Webber, 164–78. New York: Berghahn, 2007.
> Brings together the situation of sister queens and queen mothers in southern Africa, arguing that the power of these women has often been underplayed by scholars.

Carney, Elizabeth Donnelly. *Women and Monarchy in Macedonia*. Norman: University of Oklahoma Press, 2000.

Carney, Elizabeth D. and Sabine Muller eds. *The Routledge Companion to Women and Monarchy in the Ancient Mediterranean World*. London: Routledge, 2020.

> Carney is a key historian of royal women in the ancient world, particularly in the Macedonian and Hellenistic sphere—her monograph is excellent and this collection co-edited with Muller is a vital resource on queenship in the ancient world.

de la Bédoyère, Guy. *Domina: The Women who Made Imperial Rome*. New Haven: Yale University Press, 2018.

> An approachable introduction to Julio-Claudian women and early Roman empresses.

Duggan, Anne, ed. *Queens and Queenship in Medieval Europe*. Woodbridge: Boydell, 1997.

> An important collection with a selection of useful case studies, including several on Byzantium and the Latin East.

Earenfight, Theresa. "Without the Persona of the Prince: Kings, Queens and the Idea of Monarchy in Late Medieval Europe." *Gender and History* 19, no. 1 (2007): 1–21.

> A seminal article which stresses the need to look at kings and queens together as a ruling unit—highly recommended.

——. *Queenship in Medieval Europe*. New York: Palgrave Macmillan, 2013.

> Designed as a textbook, this is equally useful for students, scholars, and the wider public as a fantastic introduction to medieval European queenship.

Fleiner, Carey and Elena Woodacre, ed. *Virtuous or Villainess? The Image of the Royal Mother from the Early Medieval to the Early Modern Era*. New York: Palgrave Macmillan, 2016.

Woodacre, Elena and Carey Fleiner, ed. *Royal Mothers and their Ruling Children: Wielding Political Authority from Antiquity to the Early Modern Era*. New York: Palgrave Macmillan, 2015.

> Two linked volumes which bring together a range of case studies that stress the challenges of co-rulership between mothers and children and the power and influence of queen mothers.

Garland, Lynda. *Byzantine Empresses: Women and Power in Byzantium AD 527–1204*. London: Routledge, 1999.

> A useful survey of important Byzantine empresses from Theodora to the sack of Byzantium in the Fourth Crusade. See also the work of Judith Herrin, Liz James, and Barbara Hill.

Gillespie, Susan D. *The Aztec Kings: The Construction of Rulership in Mexica History*. Tucson: The University of Arizona Press, 1989.

> While ostensibly about Aztec kingship, this work also demonstrates the vital role of women as dynastic progenitors who provided crucial legitimation to the royal line.

Gunson, Niel. "Sacred Women Chiefs and Female 'Headmen' in Polynesian History." *The Journal of Pacific History* 22, no. 3 (1987): 139–72.

> Issues 22, nos. 3 and 4 of *JPH* are special issues on "Sanctity, Power and Gender in Polynesian History" with several articles of interest on royal women in the region.

Haeri, Shahla. *The Unforgettable Queens of Islam: Succession, Authority, Gender*. Cambridge: Cambridge University Press, 2020.

> This work looks particularly at regnant queens in Islam with studies of the Queen of Sheba, the Yemeni queens, and Razia Sultan—comparisons are made to modern politicians as well.

Hambly, Gavin R. G., ed. *Women in the Medieval Islamic World*. New York: Palgrave Macmillan, 1998.

> Despite the title, this work looks at women well into the early modern period as well—the twenty-three chapters include several excellent studies of royal women.

James, Sharon L. and Sheila Dillon, eds. *A Companion to Women in the Ancient World*. Chichester: Wiley-Blackwell, 2012.

> An excellent introduction to women's lives in the period with studies of Mesopotamian, Hellenistic, Macedonian, Egyptian, and Roman royal women.

Kaplan, Flora and S. Edouwaye, eds. *Queens, Queen Mothers, Priestesses and Power: Case Studies in African Gender*. New York: New York Academy of Sciences, 1997.

> A special issue/collection with several studies of queens and queen mothers across Africa—many are in an early modern or modern context with historical reflections.

Kosior, Katarzyna. *Becoming a Queen in Early Modern Europe*. New York: Palgrave Macmillan, 2019.

> An excellent study which offers an examination of queens in eastern Europe with comparatives across the continent and a useful focus on ceremonial.

McMahon, Keith. *Women Shall Not Rule: Imperial Wives and Concubines in China from Han to Liao*. New York: Rowman and Littlefield, 2013.

——. *Celestial Women: Imperial Wives and Concubines in China from Song to Qing*. New York: Rowman and Littlefield, 2016.

> These two volumes give an informative and entertaining introduction to Chinese empresses and royal women from the ancient era until the death of the Empress Cixi in the early twentieth century.

Mernissi, Fatima. *The Forgotten Queens of Islam*. Cambridge: Polity, 1993.

> This is a classic work on royal women in Islam which challenges perceptions that Muslim women had limited access to power and examines key examples in a thematic format.

Mukhoty, Ira. *Daughters of the Sun: Empresses, Queens and Begums of the Mughal Empire*. New Delhi: Aleph, 2018.

> An accessible overview of Mughal royal women from 1494 to 1721.

Nelson, Sarah Milledge, ed. *Ancient Queens: Archaeological Explorations*. Walnut Creek: Altamira, 2003.

A fantastic selection of case studies from an archaeological perspective which brings together fascinating examples from Asia, Europe, and the Americas.

Parsons, John Carmi, ed. *Medieval Queenship*. Stroud: Sutton, 1993.

A ground-breaking collection on royal women across Europe—Armin Wolf's survey of regnant queens and Andre Poulet's discussion of Capetian regency are particular standouts.

Peirce, Lesley. *The Imperial Harem: Women and Sovereignty in the Ottoman Empire*. Oxford: Oxford University Press, 1993.

The "go to" work on Ottoman royal women which details the workings of the harem and the women who played a vital role in politics during the "Sultanate of Women" era.

Shin, Myung-ho. *Joseon Royal Court Culture: Ceremonial and Daily Life*. Translated by Timothy V. Atkinson. Seoul: Dolbegae, 2004.

A richly informative and beautifully illustrated work—the chapters on queens including marriage, childbirth, regency, ceremonial, dress, and palatial space are highly recommended.

Stafford, Pauline. *Queens, Concubines and Dowagers: The King's Wife in the Early Middle Ages*. Leicester: Leicester University Press, 1983.

This highly respected work is an invaluable resource on early medieval queenship—its lifecycle-based approach and insightful analysis inspired generations of queenship scholars.

Tsurumi, E. Patricia. "Japan's Early Female Emperors." *Historical Reflections/Réflexions Historiques* 8, no. 1 (1981), 41–49.

A concise and informative overview of the early regnant Japanese empresses which argues that they were savvy politicians, rather than mere placeholders in times of crisis.

Walthall, Anne, ed. *Servants of the Dynasty: Palace Women in World History*. Berkeley: University of California Press, 2008.

This collection is one of the first in the field to take a global approach to women at royal courts—while not exclusively about queens, the case studies in this work are excellent.

Watanabe O'Kelly, Helen and Adam Morton, eds. *Queens Consort, Cultural Transfer and European Politics, c. 1500–1800*. London: Routledge, 2017.

This collection examines consort queens and cultural transfer across Europe—highlighting queens in Northern and Eastern Europe who are less familiar to Anglophone readers.

Woodacre, Elena, ed. *Queenship in the Mediterranean: Negotiating the Role of the Queen in the Medieval and Early Modern Eras*. New York: Palgrave Macmillan, 2013

This collection offers a range of case studies from the Iberian and Italian peninsulas, France, Byzantium and North Africa across the premodern era.

——. ed. *A Companion to Global Queenship*. Bradford: Arc Humanities, 2018.

This collection has twenty-one studies of royal women across the premodern world including comparisons between European queens and their Asian and Islamic counterparts.

Woodacre, Elena and Carey Fleiner *see* Fleiner

Printed and bound by CPI Group (UK) Ltd, Croydon, CR0 4YY

25/03/2025

14647339-0001